THE LAW OF
FAITH AND THE
BUCKING BRONCO

THE LAW OF FAITH &
THE BUCKING BRONCO

A STORY OF GOD'S WORK IN MAN, NOT MAN'S WORK FOR GOD

FRANK L. SARCONE

<u>ABOUT THE AUTHOR</u>

There is a man who goes about speaking loudly to anyone who cares to listen, throwing unfinished thoughts and ideas to the wind, just hoping that somewhere, a target was hit. Another type of man is filled with a treasure trove of golden thoughts, each syllable as valuable as the next. However, this is the man who proclaims his wisdom in whispers. His still and soft voice does no justice to the magnitude of his thoughts. It takes a wise listener to seek this voice and eagerly listen to the wonderful words that are spoken. After all, this is the one who speaks directly to the soul.

The man who wrote this book has lived a life of adventure, humor, love, and faith. His words stem from a heart so closely reflecting the heart of the God he serves and loves, and his wisdom comes from years of listening. He raised my brother and me to learn to listen, and we both share his faith because of his faithful example. I hope that his words inspire your faith too.

AUTHOR'S NOTE

Why was this book written?

A seventy-three-year-old child of God asked his Maker, "What should be my focus for the coming year?" He believed that God gave him two words: "LISTEN" and "REMEMBER." Twice each day he isolated himself to listen, without an agenda of his own. He recorded many pages of God's faithfulness, written in fragments. At the close of the year, this now seventy-four-year-old child asked the same question: "What should be my focus for the coming year?" This time he was certain he heard one word: "PROCLAIM."

This book is the proclamation of God's faithfulness and intervention. You are getting it as it was given through his times of listening and remembering. It is for whomever He has chosen to read it, but certainly, he himself was the biggest benefactor of these reflections.

***

Many thanks to my wife, Veronika, my daughter, Annaruth Chiromeras, and my daughter in-law, Kathryn Sarcone, for their many hours of work in editing and preparing this book for print.

CONTENTS

***

CHAPTER ONE : TASTE AND SEE

The Garden: Addressing man's perspective and man's energy

Genesis 1:1   In the beginning...GOD! That's all there was; He creates everything else, i.e. everything else is pure grace...

Genesis 1:27   Adam and Eve did not give themselves life – there is no boast regarding their existence, nor their morality or

Genesis 2:7   righteous character. They were given the breath (Spirit) of life. They were recipients of God's grace. And,

Genesis 1:31   God was pleased with the results. He said, "it was very good." His creation, Adam and Eve, trusted Him. How do I know that?

Hebrews 11:6   The Scripture (written/inspired by God) states: "without faith we

James 2:17   cannot please God." They could demonstrate

John 6:28-29   their faith in God by exercising it; and they did exercise faith in God's words by

Hebrews 3:18-19	staying away from the fruit of the Tree of the Knowledge of Good and Evil until the day Eve listened to another voice, and
Genesis 2:16-17	ate of the forbidden fruit, and Adam followed suit.
Revelation 12:9	By placing their faith in the serpent (the devil/Satan – Rev 12:9) violating the commandment of God,
Romans 8:1-3	they transferred from the Law of The Spirit of Life, to the Law of Sin and Death.

This was the spiritual condition, in 1974, of a firefighter, who heard an audible voice in an empty room (his bedroom) ask him: "Where are you going?

HOW WOULD YOU HAVE ANSWERED THAT VOICE?

Before discussing how the firefighter answered, let me give you a little background into his life. He had faithfully attended church until 1971, but he attended out of obligation, not enthusiasm. In fact, when grade-school age, he kept looking at the church clock anticipating the moment when he could run out of the doors and race home to catch the last fifteen minutes of a radio program that portrayed the gospel story. He did not look forward to church. At the same time, he certainly was not avoiding God either. In fact, when "The Ten Commandments" was featured in the movie theatres, he did not want to leave his seat. He wanted to watch it over and over.

Getting back to the church pew in 1971, that young boy was now a thirty-five year old off-duty New York City firefighter whose mind was wandering while seated in church. He stood up when he was supposed to, kneeled when he was supposed to and repeated memorized words and prayers when he was supposed to. Finally, he looked up and thought, almost out loud, "Is this pleasing to You? Do You like this?" He was there in body only; he knew it, and he was sure God must have known it too. The firefighter purposed to return there no more; and that's about the way it was except for attending funerals and weddings for the next three years.

That is the brief background story to the now thirty-eight year old firefighter who was between tours and catching a few winks before going back to the firehouse for a second fifteen-hour tour. It was during this brief respite that the firefighter heard an audible voice; not in his head, but to his ears, asking, "Where are you going?"

HAVE YOU CONSIDERED HOW YOU WOULD HAVE ANSWERED YET?

Well, his reply was, "I don't know where I am going, and I don't even know that You are real! If you are, it is not my job to find You, but Yours to find me."

For some reason he was spared from a bolt of lightning turning him into a cinder, but why? The only answer is GRACE. God was about to pour it out abundantly.

The firefighter went bowling with the few remaining hours before his second night tour and then proceeded to the firehouse where he picked up his gear and took the detail to a firehouse that would otherwise have been short-handed. During the course of that fifteen-hour tour, he overheard two firefighters discussing what sounded like religious issues. One of them kept using the word, "Ephesians" and also, "Colossians." When they finished conversing, our firefighter asked, "Where did you get the books you were reading from?"

One of the fellows answered, "What books?"

"You know, you mentioned one book called 'Ephesians.' "
When he said it was from the Bible, our firefighter merely gave a puzzled look and walked away, never giving it a second thought.
However, on his way home after the fifteen-hour night tour the firefighter pushed the button for some hillbilly music on his car radio, when instead, the very first word from that radio was "EPHESIANS Chapter Two, Verses Eight and Nine: For by grace you have been saved; through faith; and that not of yourselves; it is a gift of God, not as a result of works, that no one should boast." WOW!

God was still wooing, but the firefighter was still resisting. He reasoned, "Sure, heaven is free; that means Hitler is there now."
But there now was enough interest to check this thing out when he returned home. He found a Bible and using the index, opened it to Ephesians 2:8-9. To make a long story short, he chain-referenced his way from Ephesians 2:8-9 to Revelation 3:20 where he read, "I stand at the door and knock. If anyone hears my voice and opens

the door, I will come in to him and dine with him, and he with Me."

God certainly had been knocking hard on this firefighter's door, who dropped to his knees and flung the door wide open in repentance and trust. Do you know what happened to him? When he exercised faith in "The Good News" of Jesus Christ, he was not under the "Law of Sin and Death" anymore, because the "Law of the Spirit of Life in Christ Jesus" (Rom. 8:13) loosed him from the "Law of Sin and Death", and he was free! It is similar to the way that the "Law of Aerodynamics" frees us from the "Law of Gravity": It trumps it! (Romans 8:1-3).

The firefighter was given the Spirit of Life that was breathed into Adam. This was impossible to contain, and God made sure there were opportunities to pour it out. During his first tour back to work with both day crew and night crew present, someone asked, "What's new?" They got it all while it was still fresh in his mind.

There was a detail there who, returning to his own firehouse told everyone, "When you are detailed to Engine ___, ask this firefighter, 'What's new?' " He did not clarify, and they could not resist! Of course, our firefighter could not let them down either!

So, he was immediately in full-time ministry, continually exercising faith and accessing the grace of God. (Romans 5:2)

Once a bucking bronco, now a loyal steed, this firefighter loved and trusted his Master! This trust was exemplified each time he exercised his faith in God.

That is correct...faith needs to be exercised, just as the Law of Aerodynamics needs to be exercised in order to overcome gravity. We do not create the Law; we merely acknowledge and trust the Law. We trust in it every time we board an airplane. Although I have exercised this faith at times in the past, I never found cause to boast about my ability to sit on an airplane seat while it taxied me across the country. Likewise, I must exercise faith in order to access the grace expressed in the Law of the Spirit of Life in Christ Jesus! (Romans 5:2)

The transfer looks something like this:

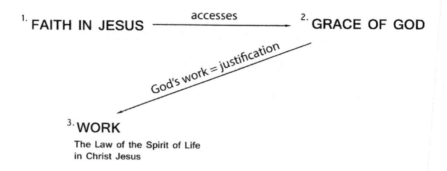

Romans 5:1-2: "Therefore having been justified freely by faith, we have peace with God through our Lord Jesus Christ through Whom also we have access by faith into His grace in which we stand, and rejoice in hope of the glory of God."

Can I boast about exercising faith? NO! Romans 3:26-28: "To demonstrate at the present time His righteousness, that He might be just and the justifier of the one who has trust in Jesus. (v.27) Where is boasting then? It is excluded. By what law? Of works? NO, but by THE LAW OF FAITH."

We have justification through the Law of Faith, but boasting is excluded because grace is God's work, and only grace can save Adam's fallen race. God justifies! He justifies through His Son!

Jesus suffered our penalty (John 3:16)- the Law of Sin and Death, (Romans 3:23) and was raised to eternal life. We are liberated from (Romans 6:23) the Law of Sin and Death through the Law of the Spirit (Ephesians 2:8-9) of Life in Christ Jesus because of His sacrifice.

We share in His suffering, and as His Body, Bride, children, we share in His resurrection. When we believe this we are called believers, when we exercise this faith in Jesus.

1 John 5:3-4 "For this is the love of God, that we keep His commandments, and His commandments are not burdensome. For whatever is born of God overcomes the world, and this is the victory that overcomes the world, our faith."

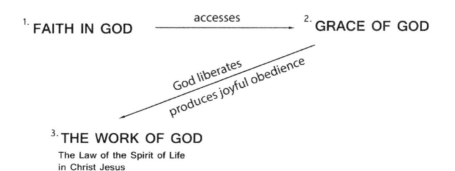

Romans 7:25   He is under a new Law, but he is not yet free from conflict from within. The old nature still beckons. He is a citizen of Heaven, but not yet home.

Have you pondered what it would take to create a totally harmonious environment? One like the Paradise promised? Someone once described heaven in terms of one giant tuning fork which sets off all the other tuning forks in the exact same frequency, i.e. perfect harmony.

Perfect harmony requires a perfect Sovereignty!

This harmony is impossible to obtain as long as we have autonomous subjects. Therefore, we read, "I will have no other gods before Me." God needs to be put first. This may sound selfish (to some) at first, but…is the cross a selfish act? God needs to be sovereign. Therefore, He says, "Don't eat of the fruit of the Tree of Knowledge of Good and Evil." For a perfectly harmonious environment, all in one accord, all accord must be HIS ACCORD because He is perfect! He gives such symbols as, one body with Christ being the head; also "I am one with the Father and you are one with Me."

THE LAW OF FAITH AND THE BUCKING BRONCO

Like a carpenter building forms so that the mason can fill them with a new concrete foundation, THE CARPENTER is building forms that He will one day fill with His Presence and we will all be one…a perfectly harmonious ONE.

The forms are being built, and when all the forms are finished and filled with the Spirit of God, a compartment of timeless space (heaven) will be secured, and its inhabitants will never experience disharmony again.

In the meantime, the Apostle Paul pens many chapters explaining our present state. He uses some laws that govern this, and sometimes uses the first person singular to illustrate it.

Paul uses the Law of Moses (The Ten Commandments) to describe perfection, and in fact, Jesus explains that the first and second commandments (when kept perfectly) are the fulfillment of all Ten Commandments! When I read the Ten Commandments I know that I have sinned and need to be rescued. If I am to love God and neighbor perfectly, I need to be changed, and things need to be different. There is no chance for utopia in the present state of our world, because of my present state and because of the present state of all of Adam's race.

One day there will be a place where perfect harmony exists because of a Sovereign God who has perfect attributes, a God Who is holy (100% pure) with no blemishes. He is orchestrating His perfect plan which includes all who exercise faith in Him.

"Exercise faith" = agree that God's way is the best way (only right way) and ask (allow) Him to accomplish it through me, the way that:

FAITH EXERCISED	**GOD DID THE REST** **(GRACE)**
Abe raised his hand with a knife in it Genesis 22:10	God gave the sacrifice Genesis 22:13-14
Moses raised his staff Exodus 14:16	God parted the Red Sea Exodus 14:21
Israel placed blood on lintels Exodus 12:7	God saved Israel's firstborn Exodus 12:23
Israel walked toward the Jordan Joshua 3:15	God made a dry path Joshua 3:16-17
Apostles waited until Pentecost Acts 1:4-14	God gave the power (H.S.) Acts 2:1-

| Hebrews 11 is a chapter illustrating faith exercised |

The Law of Faith as demonstrated in Hebrews 11

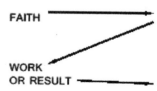

FAITH ⟶ GRACE = (1) Free Gift (2) God's ability and desire to honor faith. (3) God gives you the results of your faith.

His will for you given through your faith

WORK
OR RESULT ⟶

1 Gain approval
2 Testimony
3 Given understanding
4 Offer sacrifice
Obtain a testimony
5 Taken up with God (Enoch)
Pleasing God
6 Without faith- Can't please God
7 Obedience- build an ark
Become an heir of righteousness
8 Obedience- Go to a foreign land
9 Able to become an alien in a foreign land
10 Seek out a city God built
11 Ability, strength, power to conceive at a late age
12 Procreation
16 Desiring a better country
17 Tremendous sacrifice (Abraham and Isaac)
19 Knowing and expecting God's power
20 Trusting the promise
21 Trusting the promise
22 Trusting the promise
23 Conquering fear (Moses' mother and king's edit)
24 Loyalty- Moses refused to be called son of Pharaoh's daughter
25 Choosing ill treatment along with God's people
26 Seeing and living beyond the temporal (Moses)
27 Spiritual eyes and conquering fear
28 Not afraid to look foolish (Passover blood)
29 Expecting a miracle (Parting Red Sea)
30 Enduring (7 days around Jericho/ expecting a miracle)
31 Saved from harm (Rahab to safety)

Gain approval
11:1,5
Gain Understanding
11:3
Offer proper sacrifice
11:4
Obtain a testimony
11:4, 2
Obtain obedience
11:7, 8, 17
Strength/ Gain victory
11:9, 11, 33, 34, 12
A Heart for God and Things of God
11:16, 24, 25
Spiritual Eyes
11:10: 19, 26, 27, 29, 30
Overcome Fear
11: 23, 27
Gain Righteousness
11:7, 33
Obtained Promises
11:33
Safety
11:33, 34
Dead Restored
11:35
Trusting the Promises
11:21, 22 ,28

Others tortured and destitute
Killed in order to receive resurrection

GOD'S WORK - which was accessed as they exercised faith given them.

The Law of Faith as demonstrated in Hebrews 11

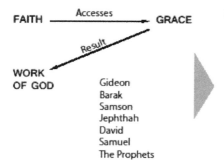

Hebrews 11: 33- 39

vs. 33   Subdued kingdoms
Worked righteousness
Obtained promises
Stopped the mouths of lions
Quenched the violence of fire
Escaped the edge of the sword
Were made strong out of weakness
Became vailiant in battle
Turned to fight the armies of aliens
Women received their dead back

All these having obtained a good testimony **through faith** did not receive the promise

vs. 36   **Others** were tortured, not accepting deliverance.
Waiting for a better resurrection

Still others- mockings, scourgings, chains, imprisonment, stoned, sawn in two, tempted

vs. 37   Slain with the sword, in sheepskins

vs. 38   They were destitute, afflicted, tormented

OF WHOM THE WORLD WAS NOT WORTHY

They wandered in deserts, in mountains, dens and caves of the earth.

An good testimony through suffering for righteousness sake.

Question: When did Job receive God's grace?
Answer : All through his period of suffering as well as before and after.
    (1) Prosperity
    (2) Suffering and loss   Grace though Faith
    (3) Prosperity

These are illustrations of men who grew in faith by exercising faith throughout their lifetime. When a plane is in flight it still needs to be applying the Laws of Flight to remain in the air. Gravity is still pulling, and constantly needs to be overcome. When I pull back on the stick I am exercising faith in the Laws of Physics.

Likewise, our firefighter learned that some habits run deeper than others. Have you ever heard the proverbial question, "How do you move a giant oak tree?" The answer is, "You move it while it is still an acorn!" Well, our firefighter had some acorns in his life, as well as a variety of different-sized saplings and oak trees that might be charted something like this:

Isaiah 61:3: "...So they may be called oaks of righteousness, the planting of the Lord, that He may be glorified."

As the trees grow, they become harder to move and leave a bigger hole when uprooted, just like a bad habit.

On the other side of the coin: good habits, when planted and nurtured, become more permanent; and living by faith (in Christ) becomes easier and we become joyfully obedient. (I John 5:3)

From Faith to Faith: The Race Car

A friend of mine wanted to become a race car driver, so he bought an expensive Corvette. He registered for a race, practiced a few laps, and then began qualifying laps with an official seated with him. The qualifier quickly recognized the novice behind the wheel and in a disgusted tone said, "Pull over; you do not deserve to own this fine automobile." He then gave him some instructions, and as they approached the first turn...at the point where my friend would ease up on the throttle...the qualifier stomped the pedal to the floor!

In a panic state, eyes bulging, my friend followed the instructions he had been given and found himself smoothly and quickly around the turn.

The same scene took place with each successive turn, including the eyes bulging, until he finally believed that the car was meant to respond just the way it had been. He not only qualified, but came in the money! His trust and follow-through resulted in joy.

Some laws are hard to exercise faith in – such as: "love your enemies", "pray for those who spitefully use you", etc. but when exercised enough you become convinced of their value, and your faith grows, and so does joy.

"FROM FAITH TO FAITH" is most literally translated "out of faith, into faith". When we exercise faith we access the grace of God. Since grace is a gift of God, we receive the result (work) from God, and it goes (back) into increasing the faith that was exercised, thereby accessing more grace (Romans 1:17).

The idea is to form those good habits, i.e. get those acorns in the ground early, nurturing them to grow into steadfast giant oak trees, by faith in God.

The firefighter's life was not problem-free (Psalm 34:19) , but he learned that trials are not only allowed, but some are designed by God to help the process of faith-building and spiritual growth (1 Peter 1:7).

PAGES 19-27 ARE ADDED TO SUPPORT THESE CONCEPTS WITH SCRIPTURE.

What is Faith?

"Now faith is the assurance of things hoped for, the conviction of things not seen." Hebrews 11:1

The Premise: When I am not acting out God's will (The Truth) in faith, I am trusting in a lie. The person who is not trusting Jesus for his salvation, is actively trusting in a lie!

The Proof-Text: We can place our faith in a lie (deception) and thereby follow that lie!

Proverbs 14:12 "There is a way which seems right to a man, but its end is the way of death."

Hebrews 3:13 "But encourage one another day after day, as long as it is still called 'today', lest anyone of you be hardened by the deceitfulness of sin."

Galatians 6:3 "For if anyone thinks he is something when he is nothing, he deceives himself."

Romans 1:21b…"But they became futile in their speculations, and their foolish heart was darkened."

Romans 1:22 "Professing to be wise, they became fools."

Actions must follow true faith:

James 1:22 "But prove yourselves doers of the word, not merely hearers who delude themselves."

James 2:14 "What use is it, my brethren, if a man says he has faith, but he has no works? Can that faith save him?"

James 2:17 "Even so faith, if it has no works, is dead, being by itself."

James 2:18 (The key) "But someone may well say, 'you have faith, and I have works; show me your faith without the works, and I will show you my faith by my works." (Your actions display what you really believe to be true).

20

James 2:22 "You see that faith was working with his works (actions) and as a result of the works (actions) faith was perfected."

James 2:24 "You see that a man is justified by works, and not by faith alone." (Because faith alone, that is, faith without actions, is not faith at all.)

James 2:26 "For just as the body without the spirit is dead, so faith without works is dead." (A dead faith is no faith!)

If you believe in a lie, you will be carrying out the works of that lie. If you believe in the truth, you will be carrying out the works of the truth!

Examples of Practicing Faith:

Hebrews 11:3 "By faith we understand that the worlds were prepared by the word of God, so that what is seen was not made out of things which are visible."

How does this faith get acted out in life?

What if your faith was in "evolution"?

How does your faith affect your world-view?

How does your world-view affect your behavior?

Hebrews 11:8 By faith Abraham, when he was called, obeyed by going out to a place which he was to receive for an inheritance; and he went out, not knowing where he was going."

Obedience is always implied in regard to faith.

Actions follow faith.

The Law of Faith:

We have been justified through the law of faith.

Romans 3:26-28 "To demonstrate at the present time His righteousness, that He might be just and the justifier of the one who has trust in Jesus. Where is boasting then? It is excluded. By what law? Of works? No, but by the law of faith." NKJ

James 2:23 "And the scripture was fulfilled which says, Abraham believed God and it was accounted to him for righteousness. And he was called the friend of God."
Faith gives access to grace.

Romans 5:1-2 "Therefore, having been justified freely by faith, we have peace with God through our Lord Jesus Christ, through whom also we have access by faith into His grace in which we stand, and rejoice in the hope of the glory of God."

Here, works are synonymous with faith.

John 6:28-29 "Then they said to Him, what shall we do that we may work the works of God? Jesus answered and said to them, this is the work of God, that you believe in Him whom He sent." Here, unbelief, is a synonym for disobedience.

Hebrews 3:18-19 "And to whom did He swear that they would not enter His rest, but to those who did not obey? (19) So we see that they could not enter in because of unbelief."

Again, faith and works are synonymous.

James 2:17-18 "Thus also faith by itself, if it does not have works, is dead. But someone will say, you have faith, and I have works. Show me your faith without your works, and I will show you my faith by my works."

Living is an action. Faith becomes an action.

Habakkuk 2:4 "Behold the proud, his soul is not upright in him, but the just shall live by his faith."

Mark 9:23 "Jesus said to him, if you believe, all things are possible to him who believes."

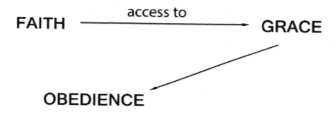

Faith accesses God's grace, and God's grace causes obedience. Salvation comes by grace through faith (Ephesians 2:8-9), and sanctification (godly living) comes via faith (i.e. faith in God/God's truth). Habakkuk 2:4, Romans 1:17

Faith (in God) is contrasted with faulty reasoning (your own understanding),

Proverbs 3:5-6 "Trust in the Lord with all your heart and lean not on your own understanding; in all your ways acknowledge Him and He will direct your paths."

Proverbs 14:12 "There is a way that seems right to a man, but it's way is the way of death."

James 1:22 "But be ye doers of the Word and not just hearers only, deceiving your own selves."

Following our own understanding leads to self-deception (believing a lie.)

1 John 1:8 "If we say that we have no sin, we deceive ourselves, and the truth is not in us."

Faith is the antidote to self-deception (faulty reasoning)

2 Corinthians 5:7 "For we walk by faith, not by sight."

Gentiles were given access to faith, which gives them access to grace.

Acts 14:27 "And when they were come, and had gathered the church together, they reviewed all that God had done with them, and how He had opened the door of faith to the Gentiles."

Acts 15:9 "And put no difference between us and them, purifying their hearts by faith."

Faith is absolutely necessary to access the grace of God.

Romans 14:23: "And he who doubts is condemned if he eats, because he does not eat from faith; for whatever is not from faith is sin."

Hebrews 4:2 "For unto us was the gospel preached, as well as unto them, but the word preached did not profit them, not being mixed with faith in them that heard it."

Hebrews 11:6 "But without faith it is impossible to please Him, for he that comes to God must believe that He is, and that He is a rewarder of them that seek Him."

Matthew 8:13 "...As you have believed, so let it be done to you."

Matthew 17:19 "…Why couldn't we cast it out?...(20) because of unbelief."

Mark 6:4-6 "Jesus could only heal a few people in Nazareth because of their unbelief."

Mark 9:23 "…All things are possible to him who believes."

Mark 10:52 "…Go your way, your faith has made you well."

Mark 11:24 "…When praying, believe and you will receive."

Continually entertaining a certain lie can lead to accepting it as true and obeying it, leading to the problems at the bottom left on the following chart. Finding the truth of the matter and continuing can produce the bottom right side of the chart.

COUNSELING MODEL

FAITH

IN A LIE
Wisdom from Below

MOTIVATES

IN THE TRUTH
Wisdom from above

Entertaining
a Lie

ACCEPTANCE

OF THE LIE
Reliance upon self

MOTIVATES

OF THE TRUTH
Reliance upon God

Accepting
it as truth

OBEDIENCE

TO THE LIE
Fruits of Selfishness
guilt, anxieties, lusts, broken relationships

TO THE TRUTH
Fruits of the Spirit

CHAPTER TWO: GOD MOVES IN STRANGE WAYS

The firefighter was a single man who enjoyed riding his motorcycle. Returning home from a ride in a deserted section of town, as he made a gradual bend in the road, barricades appeared blocking his path. The only recourse was a quick left turn. Unfortunately the pavement was coated with oil, and it was impossible to stay upright. His left leg was under the bike while it ended its skid to a stop.

With no one around, cell phones not yet invented, and a damaged leg, he headed home. When he was heading south, his handle-bars were pointing east. On his way home he pondered the circumstance.

He thought aloud, "There is nothing I did to cause this result. God could have put the thought in my mind to take a different route home. He certainly was aware of the hazard I encountered, and He allowed it to happen, whether He designed it or not. Therefore, there is something to learn from this, BUT WHAT?"

There was the excitement of anticipation, but no direction whatsoever. He pulled out his Bible and searched for clues. Hours went by, and suddenly one passage of Scripture jumped off the page: "FAITH WITHOUT WORKS IS DEAD". There was a confirmation in his heart that he had the answer to God's purpose, but still had no clue how to apply it, or what the will of God was in this situation, when suddenly the phone rang. His leg was racked with pain as he hobbled his way to the phone.

It was a fellow firefighter who had never before called, and with whom he had never played tennis; but that's exactly what he wanted to do. Our firefighter's thoughts were, "I can't; I am busy tomorrow (he did not want to acknowledge his damaged leg to anyone yet) but since he was reluctant to lie, he paused, and during that pause the words, "faith without works is dead" flashed into his mind.

His heart pounded as he realized this was the application for him. He thought, *God wants to heal me*, and answered the friend, "How about 9:30AM? I will get there at 9:00 to sign us in." Our firefighter knew that this was not the context of the Scripture, "faith without works is dead", but he also was certain enough that God was using it to get him to exercise faith and he would be willing to chase the first ball served to him, no matter what!

The leg was mega-swollen and multi-colored when he went to sleep, but it looked and felt every bit as good as his right leg when he awakened in the morning. He signed up for two players at 9:00 AM, but the other player never showed up.

May I ask you…are you surprised about this?

My next question to you would be: "Why?" Why are we taken back by testimonies like this?

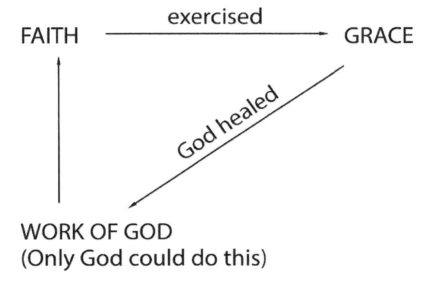

FAITH ——— exercised ——→ GRACE

God healed

WORK OF GOD
(Only God could do this)

"For momentary light affliction is producing for us an eternal weight of glory far beyond all comparison." (2 Corinthians 4:17-18)

"While we look not at the things which are seen; for the things which are seen are temporal, but the things which are not seen are eternal." (Romans 1:17)

"The just shall live by faith."

When we believe that God is always there for us, even when we cannot see Him working to relieve our trial, we are exercising our faith and thereby growing in faith.

Hebrews 11:1 says, "Now faith is the assurance of things hoped for, the conviction of things not seen."

The late Martin Lloyd Jones once wrote: "The only time Biblical faith can be exercised is when we cannot see God work on our behalf."

Therefore, we can rejoice at the opportunities to exercise faith and thereby grow in faith when we continue to trust that He is working things out for the best, whatever that might be. (1 Corinthians 10:13)

The Law of Faith

God is just; are you surprised?
Do you feel cheated from His grace?

He sent His own dear Son to die.
He suffered in your place.

You who feel such burden,
You who feel such shame.

So you could then be free from sin,
So you could bear His name.

To ones who can't take credit
By works that they have done.

Who trust despite the trials of life,
The finished work of His dear Son.

He demonstrates His righteousness,
And shows that He is just.

His "Law of Faith" removes all boast,
It credits only those who trust.

This earth is not your final rest,
Don't look for heaven here.

Circumstance will pull and test
And He will not seem always near.

Let trusting be your shelter.
Let trusting set you free.

Trust is never trust at all
Unless you trust what you can't see!
TRUST JESUS!

Frank L. Sarcone

CHAPTER THREE: THE LOVE PARADIGM

I Corinthians 13 is often read to the bride and groom at wedding ceremonies because it describes the perfect love relationship. There is only one Groom who gives unfailing love to His Bride. Jesus does not give to His Bride out of responsibility or gain; He gives from a pure motive of love (John 3:16).

Salvation is a gift of love to whoever trusts in Him with their lives. To each of these believers He gives a measure of faith (Romans 12:3; Hebrews 12:2), but as we have learned, faith without actions is no faith at all.

When our firefighter fell to his knees in repentance and surrendered to the will of God (Galatians 5:6), he exercised the faith given him, and received grace (the fruit of God's love) toward salvation. He was given justification when he exercised his faith in God and in God's truth.

Now he was experiencing God's faithfulness with each act of faith. Reading the Gospels (Luke 24:13) was like being in the company of Jesus. After walking the Emmaus Road he would wipe the dust from his clothing while his heart warmed within him. (Luke 24:13) He could smell the fish that fed the three thousand, and the five thousand (Matthew 14:15). He could be astounded with the twelve while their nets were overflowing, (Luke 5:6) and when the sea was calmed by mere words from the mouth of Jesus (Matthew 8:26). How can anyone put this book (the Bible) down? To top it all off, Jesus told His apostles they would be even better off when He departs to be with the Father, because The Holy Spirit would come down upon them to live within each believer (John 14:26, Acts 1:8). "That's me!" the firefighter said, "a believer!" Life was never this exciting!

He hung upon every word that came out of the mouth of God. Oh what lessons he learned from God's truths, especially from some of the hard sayings, such as "Love your enemies", "Pray for those who despitefully use you" (Matthew 5:44).

On his way to work one morning, he stopped at a full stop sign, but the car behind him did not attempt to stop. Instead, while on two wheels it climbed the curb to his right and swung a screeching turn in front of our firefighter who had just begun to move forward. A mosquito would not have fit within the allowed space of the two cars! Yesterday he knew the principle, "love your enemies", but today he had an opportunity to exercise it.

The firefighter thought, "The driver needs a beating"; however, God knew he needed prayer. He heard the words, "Pray for him". Well, it was not exactly a joyful obedience. He began something like "Lord keep the bum from killing somebody", but as he continued to pray he heard the sirens from his own company leaving quarters, and he began to wonder if the driver's family might be in need. Maybe that is why he drove like a maniac.

God was changing his heart toward the driver, and his prayers became in earnest for the driver and his family. He was able to hear the wee small voice of God above the shouting of self.

Self wanted quick retribution; but God wanted ministry... and ministry He got! Instead of bitterness and agita, the firefighter was at peace in his heart, and actually felt like an instrument of God. It was becoming more and more clear that success had nothing to do with his own ability to perform, but it had everything to do with his growing and developing trust in God and His word. God is pleased when He sees faith in action. There was a relationship going on. It was a caring relationship even though there was *no* question regarding who was Master and who was servant! The firefighter knew that was the only way it could be, and certainly the way it should be.

Poem

Inspired by C.S. Lewis and A.W. Tozer

The body with its soul

Peers through a fleshly grid.

It ponders human logic to perform.

Ah, but the soul that has a body

The Spirit does control.

And a life that's lived by faith

Becomes the norm.

Frank L. Sarcone

COUNSELING MODEL 2

FAITH

IN A LIE
Wisdom from Below

"Who does he think he is?"
"I have my rights!"
"He needs a beating!"

IN THE TRUTH
Wisdom from above

Love your enemies.
Pray for those persecute you.

Let it grow in this soil

MOTIVATES

ACCEPTANCE

OF THE LIE
Reliance upon self

OF THE TRUTH
Reliance upon God

MOTIVATES

OBEDIENCE

TO THE LIE
Fruits of Selfishness

Would have grown to anger, bitterness, depression

TO THE TRUTH
Fruits of the Spirit

The bronco was being tamed, and he was a one-rider horse. He pondered, "When the rider is God, there is no room for doubting. Doubts are irrational." Our firefighter once asked a non-believer (who was diagnosed with clinical anxiety) the following question, "If you had a friend with no limitations, there is nothing he cannot accomplish, he has almighty, miraculous abilities, and he loves you even more than his own life, do you believe you would have the same anxieties? He answered, "No, how could I?" How much more a believer?

Because our firefighter wanted God to have the reins, the listening side of prayer was most intriguing. It usually required stillness (a quiet spirit), but as he prayerfully read his Bible, he was reluctantly being led toward church attendance and involvement. The lone ranger was doing just fine. Why in the world would he want to join a stable full of horses? But, true to suit he reasoned, "God said it. I believe it. And that's good enough for me!" Nonetheless he voiced his protest, "Alright, but if you find me a church like this one..." as he pointed to the book of Acts in the Bible.

The bronco still had some buck in him, but the rider had a firm but gentle hand on the reins and off they went to church. He began ministry as an usher. But you can't be giving violations on

Monday for unlawful assembly and putting chairs in the aisles in church on the following Sunday! But what can you do? What should you do? It seemed God was saying, "Make your appeals, pray, and keep it to yourself!"

There were seven such things on his prayer list. The firefighter's face lights up with a broad smile when he recounts how several months later, with the opening of the new church extension, he was approached by the associate pastor with a request. The request included seven new areas of responsibility. His heart almost burst with song, "What a Mighty God We Serve", as he crossed off his list of seven prayers, one by one!

It is here that our firefighter realizes, "as long as I continue to exercise faith in Almighty God, I will never cease to be astounded!"

FAITH THAT ——— accesses ———▶ **GOD'S GRACE**
GOD'S WAY IS BEST

God did the work & permitted him to be part of the cure

GOD'S WORK
The Law of the Spirit of Life
in Christ Jesus

Poem

The Bucking Bronco

The bucking bronco bucks

To loose the Rider from its reins.

It lets no shackle limit or restrain. (Psalm 2)

It doesn't view the pitfalls

As it prances on its way.

It cannot see the crevice on the plain.

But the Rider has been this way before,

Knows every inch of turf along the way.

The reins can be your safety net

To keep the grass beneath your feet.

It is best for you to let the Rider stay.

Frank L. Sarcone

CHAPTER FOUR: GUARDING THE TRUTH

His mind was being renewed (Romans 12:2). The renewed mind does not just learn God's principles, but *interprets life through them.* He began to view people and events in a different light. His character was changing. God's character does not change, nor does His Word. He is immutable, and He is consistent with His Word. The more time the firefighter spent in God's word the easier it became to distinguish His consistent voice (1Ki.19:12). Like the prophet Elijah, "the wee-small voice" of God was being recognized over the noisy storm. Life can muffle truth with its many distractions.

Religious leaders are not immune to these temptations. The Jewish leaders were to be keepers of "The Truth", but they were blocking out the words of Jesus Christ (John 8:37-38). The word, "xopew" (coreo) along with a negative, indicates that they made no room for the words of Jesus. Their personal positions would not allow it. The boundaries of truth must extend to every word out of the mouth of God. Sometimes boundaries of truth are narrowed by the doctrinal positions of well-meaning men, and these positions are treated as objective facts by their followers. Consider the charts on the following pages:

BOUNDARIES OF TRUTH

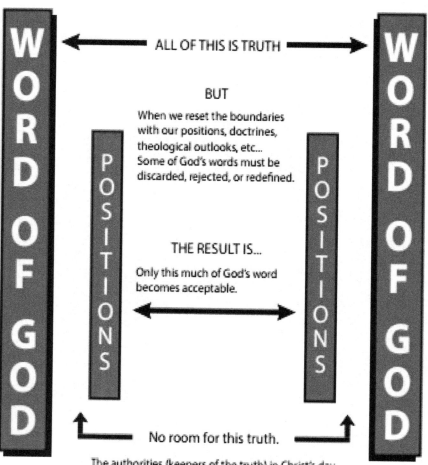

← ALL OF THIS IS TRUTH →

BUT

When we reset the boundaries with our positions, doctrines, theological outlooks, etc... Some of God's words must be discarded, rejected, or redefined.

THE RESULT IS...

Only this much of God's word becomes acceptable.

No room for this truth.

The authorities (keepers of the truth) in Christ's day had no room for His words when His words reached outside of their biblical positions.
Our firefighter reasoned,

WHAT ABOUT THE THEOLOGIANS OF TODAY, ARE THEY IMMUNE?

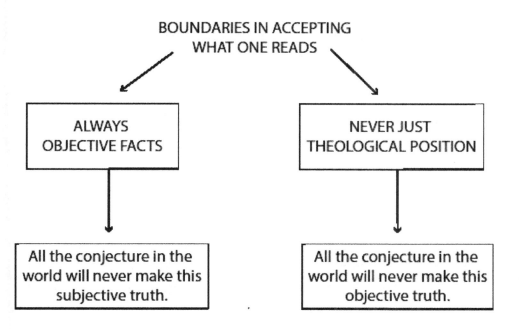

Jesus' words may, at times, look subjective as He quotes scripture in a different way than the religious leaders did in some circumstances, but, being God makes it objective. Likewise, the writers of scripture, under divine guidance from the Holy Spirit spoke objectively because it was from God.. God is truth, and therefore what He says is fully objective.

Be aware which column you can conjecture from!

<u>Processional caterpillar</u>

When he was a young boy, our firefighter observed a procession as he was sitting alone on the pavement in front of his residence. He recalls spotting a procession of caterpillars circling a telephone pole. Non-stop, nose-to-tail, the procession went on and on. He had never seen that many caterpillars in one place before, let alone a string of them in a tight circle. More than thirty years later, he learned that caterpillars were so processional that whenever a line of them needs to detour around an obstruction, the leader (locomotive) may catch sight of the trailer (caboose) and follow it wherever it goes. So the procession begins and direction is lost. This procession will never cease without intervention. Caterpillars have been known to starve to death rather than leave the procession, even for food that is within sight.

Someone once said, without absolute, objective truth, like caterpillars we are prone to follow some leaders who are part of a circle going nowhere.

Proverbs 14:12: "There is a way that seems right to a man but its end is the way of death."

A human being – a person of the world

Humanity - every person in the world

Humanism - a philosophy of the world that opposes the will of God

The following chart is a comparison between the Bible's truth and the statements found in 1973's *The Humanist Manifesto I and II.* (Edited by Paul Kurtz.)

THE BIBLE	MIDDLE GROUND	HUMANIST MANIFESTO I
Genesis 1:1 "God created the heavens and the earth."	T H E R E	"We therefore affirm the following: P.8-10 11. P1: "The universe is self-existing, not created."
Genesis 1:27 "God created man in His image."	I S	P2. Man is part of nature, he has emerged (evolved)
I Timothy 2:13 Woman is from man, not vice versa. "For Adam was first formed, then Eve."	N O N E	P5. Science makes unacceptable any supernatural or cosmic guarantee of human values.
Romans.9:20 "O man! Who are you, anyway, to talk back to God? The thing that is being molded does not say to the one who molds it, 'Why do you make me this way', does it?"		#6. The time has passed for deism. #11 These views should be fostered by education and supported by custom.

THE BIBLE	MIDDLE GROUND	HUMANIST MANIFESTO II
Proverbs 20:24 "A man's steps are ordered by the LORD; how then can man understand his way?"	T H E R E	#10 No belief in supernatural.
Galatians 1:8 "But even if we or an angel from heaven should preach to you a gospel that differs from what we have preached, to you, a curse on him." Isaiah 10:15 "Should an axe boast itself over the man who hews with it, or a saw vaunt itself over the one who moves it back and forth?	I S N O N E	#13 Religious institutions must be reconstituted.
Ezekiel 18:4 "Observe! All souls are Mine; the soul of the father as well as the soul of the son is Mine; it is the person that sins who shall die."		# 10 last paragraph: Man alone is responsible and has the power for achievement. #16 We begin with humans, not God.

THE BIBLE	MIDDLE GROUND	HUMANIST MANIFESTO II
Job 21:22 "Can anyone teach God knowledge? It is He who judges those on high."	T H E R E	#18: Human ethics = anything goes; promiscuity is encouraged.
Psalm 127:1 "Unless the LORD builds the house, their labor is futile who build it. Unless the LORD preserves the city, the sentry watches in vain."	I S N O N E	#19: Freedom of speech, euthanasia, right to suicide. #21: A system of world law and order.
John 1:1: "In the beginning was the Word, and the Word was with God, and the Word was God."		#21: Planet earth must be considered a single ecosystem.
Acts 4:12 "And there is salvation through no one else; for there is no other name under heaven given among		

men by which we must be saved." Provers 6:32: "He who commits adultery is lacking in sense, and he who does it is destroying himself."		

CHAPTER FIVE: GOD'S SENSE OF HUMOR

When you take God at His word people begin to notice. Some seem rather offended. Others take note and keep an eye on your life. God seems to have fun with the latter.

On a certain Sunday evening, individually, two young ladies approached our firefighter with pretty much the same cry, "I can't tolerate my boss any longer." To the first one he said, "It's best to leave a job from a position of strength. Why not purpose to do things that make your boss look good?" Then they got on their knees and prayed that God would make it easy for her to do. The next time our firefighter saw her, her eyes were aglow with utter amazement at the omnipotent, caring God she met on Monday morning. Her boss was fifteen feet in front of her after going through the turntable glass doors into the vast lobby of their office building. It was on that spot that his heart stopped and he collapsed to the marble floor. Our young lady was "Johnny on the Spot" with her CPR skills, and he lived to appreciate her like never before!

The second young lady was given the same advice and the same prayer, asking God to make her attempts to make her boss look good easy and effective. She was at her desk on Monday morning astounded at the grateful boss who had just left her office. He warmly thanked her for a card that read, "I missed you while you were on vacation; it is really good to have you back." She meant that card for her friend's desk, who was also on vacation, but somehow God had better use of it. Who knew? God knew!

God also knew that our firefighter's brother was looking over his shoulder. They had built a two-family home together. The firefighter's mother lived with him on the second floor, and his brother and family lived on the first floor. There was a door that was never locked, giving access from one side to the other. Our firefighter, returning from a church picnic organized by his singles group, found his brother perched at that door. He had been listening to weather stations reporting that there was not a dry patch of land within miles of the deluged, metropolitan area, yet he was certain the firefighter and his church were high and dry all day. He stayed at the door to prove this to his family. Pointing to his wife and four kids he said to the firefighter, "Tell them how the picnic went!" Then he shouted, "See, I told you so!" His faith was growing as he watched God in his brother's life, and not many days later our firefighter had a kindred spirit

living in the same house. Shortly after that they both had a
mother acknowledging Jesus as her Lord and Savior.

WHAT A MIGHTY GOD WE SERVE!

In like manner, some of his firefighter buddies were looking
over their shoulders. There was a gasoline shortage. When
fortunate enough to find a gas station that was pumping you
would become part of a huge line of cars hoping there would be
some gasoline left when you finally arrived at the pump. Our
firefighter's company found a way to overcome this. They
would go to the head of the line with the rig and fill the gasoline
cans they stored. When returning to quarters this gasoline,
which they paid for, was emptied into their personal cars. Our
firefighter's gas tank read "E" for effort, but he did not believe
God would want him jumping a line, so he did not share in the
booty. One buddy thought he figured out a way to help out. He
said to our firefighter, "I got it figured out. You take the gas
that I siphon from my gas tank, and I'll pour the stuff that you
won't take, because of your conscience, into my car." When
our firefighter declined, that buddy said to everyone about to
leave quarters, "I don't have a clue how, but I just know that
God is going to get him a tank of gasoline!" His faith was
honored! Our firefighter knew he would be fortunate enough to
get home on the mere fumes left in his gas tank, let alone get

back to work the next day. But there came that "wee small voice" again. It said, "go home another way." The bronco began bucking again, thinking, "It's a wild goose chase, and I may run out of gas taking the long way home." But the wee small voice won out. He had the last watch so he had his uniform shirt on. He passed a station that looked closed with no cars in it, but he came this far so he thought he might as well inquire what day the pumps would be open. The owner said, "You're a firefighter aren't you? Well look at this new circular that just came in. Emergency workers will be prioritized even if off duty, and given gasoline, only if in uniform." Our firefighter got a private filling from an otherwise closed gas station. How does one handle such love without his heart bursting through his chest? Guess who was waiting for him the next morning at the watch desk? That's right, and guess the first words out of his mouth? That's right, "God got you gas, right?"

God is very visible to those who have eyes to see!

CHAPTER SIX: HE RESTORETH MY SOUL

Firefighting was fun, and working with guys like this made it like family fun. When working on a fire, you did not need to look behind you. You could trust your back to these guys. You came to know their wives and kids through company outings which drew you even closer together.

It also made the pain much greater; playing ping pong with a buddy at 11 P.M. and working feverishly to restore his life at a shipyard fire at 4 A.M., then picking up the outside phone upon returning to quarters only to hear his wife's voice asking where he might be. And shortly after that your officer goes down while you are fighting a lumber yard blaze. These events, our firefighter said, happened "B.C." By that he meant "Before Christ", i.e. before he received Christ into his life. There will always be pain and grief on occasions like this, but there are other factors present when you call upon the Lord.

Again, it was the wee hours of the morning, but this time it was an apartment building. His company should have been standing by, but somehow our firefighter made the fire floor where he carried out a toddler who was hiding behind floor length curtains after playing with matches that caused the blaze. It was too late for both he and his brother. The wailing of the parents and the lingering image of the little face bore heavy on our firefighter's heart. He did not go straight home from work. He just kept driving anywhere and nowhere. When he finally entered his bedroom he flopped to his knees in prayer. Words came out that he did not understand. They were coming out of his mouth rapidly, and as they came out peace was flooding his soul. Nothing like this had ever happened to him before, but he sure would not mind if it happened again.

He slept well that night.

1Corinthians 14:2 "For the person who speaks in a tongue does not speak to men but to God, for no one understands him; however in the Spirit he speaks mysteries."

Psalm 139:1-2: "Lord, You have searched me and known me. You know when I sit down and when I stand up. You understand my thoughts from far away."

CHAPTER SEVEN: HE TAKES ME AS I AM, AND USES ME

When asked what gives him the most excitement in life our firefighter says, "I want you to conjecture with me for a moment or two." Then he asks you to consider a pastor praying for his homosexual son. It is 9 A.M., about the time our firefighter is leaving quarters after a night tour. He is chomping at the bit to do something, but does not know what, so he says, "Lord, take me somewhere." Then he drives until he comes to the dead end of a street. There is nothing but beach in front of him. He walks the deserted beach until he sees some young folk about to push off on a sailboat. They were not considering the wind direction and would have piled up on the rocks east of them. He helps them out, but he is certain that he was taken there for a different reason. He walks some more. Time goes by without anything significant taking place, so he heads toward his parked car.

Within two hundred yards of his car he sees a lone figure lingering by it. He is certain that this is his mission. The young man wanted to pick him up, so he started a conversation by asking our firefighter, "What's that book in your back pocket?" It was the Late Great Planet Earth, which started the conversation in the direction God wanted it to go. This man's sole defense for the sin he was practicing was, "God made us in such a way that it is impossible for a man not to have sexual relief." God could have found many Christians better qualified to lecture this man on this subject, but where else would he find someone in his thirties who was available and was living it, i.e. single and celibate, probably at the time someone was praying for him? Our firefighter drove home saying over and over, "How does God do that?"

Our learner becomes a teacher

Our firefighter chose a young man and a young lady from his singles group at church to teach a weekly, new believers class with him. The young lady, a true kindred spirit, would one day become his bride.

What stories these new believers would tell of the steadfast saints in their lives! Those who kept giving love even while their Bible pages were being glued together, or while pot was being blown in their faces, or even lives being threatened. These were stories that put our firefighter to shame, as he recalls a contrasting story of his own. One he learned a great lesson from.

His church was to demonstrate its appreciation for policemen on a certain Sunday morning. There was a police officer living across the street from our firefighter, but he was not the type to come anywhere near his church. So, why invite him? Well, guess who went forward to learn more about Jesus? And guess who was waiting for him at the altar (with a smirk and with egg all over his face) when he arrived? His neighbor was soon to become a regular member of his congregation.

God eventually sealed this lesson by bringing our firefighter's attention to the account of a Samaritan woman drawing water from a well (John 4). In a brief conversation with Jesus she came to believe that He was the Messiah. She excitedly bolted off to tell her village folk of the good news. Apparently though, she lost some nerve as she looked into the faces of her townsmen because she was expecting a negative reply to her question: "This couldn't be the Messiah, could it?" But despite her apparent fear, she did speak, and they did listen, and they did follow, and they did see and taste for themselves, and our firefighter did get a lesson from a once wayward woman!

School Days

What is the Biblical approach when the bride's oldest brother, a sister, and their families refuse to share in the celebration of your wedding "in that church"? You bring them wedding cake on the wettest, umbrella-wrecking day of the year with wedding train blowing like a kite tail, and gown stuck to your body. That's the kind of gal our firefighter married!

She married a firefighter in the process of retirement. They gave the fire department pension to support his mom. He was headed toward a Bible College degree, was installed as an elder with the responsibility of Pastoral Care in his church, and was doing wedding photography to pay for college.

He began by taking liberal arts classes in a local college. The opening statement of his biology professor was, "This is a science course, and that idiot President (of the USA) and his cohorts will not infiltrate this classroom with his nonsense about creation." This was spoken before giving his name, or even saying 'hello' to his class!

What an eye-opener this was! The school was a good place for missionaries! Our firefighter loved a good fight, but God said, "We don't fight souls; we win souls!" So he sat on his hands until he was told to raise them. What he learned from this was the best part of his college education. God set the stage and the timing. He got a new definition for confronting in love. By midterm the classroom dynamic changed whenever the professor left his/her expertise and discussed values or religious beliefs. Students began speaking up on behalf and in defense of their family values, religions, and beliefs, and it was all being done in a friendly demeanor. Instead of an adversary, some teachers began to recognize our firefighter as an advocate. In one class (American History), our firefighter was asked to explain the difference in denominations, and how they came about. In biology, the whole chapter regarding evolution was skipped over. In English Literature, he could discuss the philosophy of Christian authors. In Astronomy he explained his view on origins. In a History of Christianity class he gave an oral report on the book of Hebrews. In Public Speaking, one student challenged him to debate the abortion/pro-life positions. During the debate that student kept saying, "Wow, I didn't know that!" Students were seeing options, and by the midterm many were ready to stand tall for their beliefs. One young lady, a preacher's kid, thanked him for the renewed courage she found and intended to continue to exercise. She was now exercising faith, and loving it!

However, it wasn't the students or the professors that were learning the most. It was our firefighter! Left to his own, natural methods he would have been just another rebel in just another classroom who would have eventually been exposed through classroom dynamics. Given enough time a class of students will not only hear the words you speak, but they will also begin to evaluate the person speaking those words. What you are *becoming* is even more important than what you are saying or *doing*!

Sometimes students inquired, "How do you maintain your intellectual interest when you don't agree with a certain text book?" He would say, "I picture a scene where an apple, an orange, and an apple pie are being carefully inspected. After poking and sniffing, the absolute decision is made. The pie came from the orange!!! With this in mind the apple is discarded. Thereafter, any mention of the apple brings discredit and disfavor. The stimulation comes as I marvel at the creativity and intellect that can take an orange and make it feel and smell and taste *almost* like an apple pie, and wait in faith for the next generation of scientists to finally prove the pie's origin.

CHAPTER EIGHT: BEHIND THE SCENES

If we were to choose one-word definitions for the consequences of Adam and Eve's fall (sin), they would be: "pain", "toil", and "death". Guess who our firefighter found to be most attentive to the Good News? That is correct. When medicine cannot relieve your pain, when you aren't able to put food on the table, when doctors have no encouragement for your terminal illness, your ears prick up toward the eternal God! You become a much better listener. God uses the consequences of sin to draw people back to Him.

Look with me behind the scenes.

Visitation

Our firefighter was becoming busy with hospital visitation. Whenever God ministered *through* our firefighter He always used the opportunity to minister *to* our firefighter.

One such conversation went something like this: "Lord, I am driving to a hospital to visit an old school buddy. Don't You think it would be beneficial to have the gift of evangelism? I've been visiting at these hospitals for months now, and I don't see people beating down the gates of heaven to get in. You did place me in this ministry. Where is the fruit?" God somehow set the stage to answer this question before it was ever put forth; in fact, before it was even formulated in the firefighter's mind. How else would his school buddy's sister be smack in front of the firefighter as he exited the elevator? She excitedly said, "I'm so glad to see you! You have to talk with my brother!"

He replied, "About what?"

She said, "You know, the Lord, just as you spoke to my daughter in this same hospital. I pretended that I wasn't listening, but when you left I hurried to the drawer with the Bible and looked at those verses you recited, and at my daughter's wake I kneeled at her casket and asked Jesus to be my Lord and Savior. Please talk with my brother." The firefighter answered, "That's why I came!"

Upon entering the room as lunch was being served, our firefighter asked God to please remove the three relatives who were at the bedside and they promptly left. While feeding him soup, our firefighter asked, "Do you remember the last time we spoke?" He answered, "Sure, you came to my office in the city and we went out for lunch. You said I was reading everything but the best all-time seller."

"And?"

"Well, I bought myself a Bible. I read it cover to cover, and I asked Jesus to be my Lord and Savior. I know I have a terminal illness, but I know one day I'll open my eyes and look into the face of my Savior."

"Why are you keeping it such a secret?"

"Well, every time I talked with my family they just said, 'Sure, it's just another new phase he is going through.' "

On the return trip there was one overwhelmed, grateful firefighter who was all choked up with the awesome love of God. All he could say was, "Lord, I'm sorry. I should have known! I don't need to see behind the scenes anymore, but it sure is encouraging when I do!"

Know Why You Are There: Get To The Point

An upbeat, young priest was encouraging a young man in a hospital bed, worn down to skin and bone by an AIDS virus. "Come on guy, the team needs their coach back on the field.

Hang tough man, we've got to get you home soon." Those were the parting words that our firefighter heard from the hall as he waited for a moment of privacy with the man someone had asked him to visit.

After a brief introduction to the man and his wife, our firefighter asked, "Are you confident in your relationship with God?"

"No, not at all!"

"Do you want to be?"

"Absolutely!"

The room was soon filled with tears of repentance and the joy of forgiveness. Two months later the man's wife hurried to our firefighter, who was in the hospital emergency room for another visit. The man had died during the same week of the visitation, she exclaimed. In his final moment, he had a smile on his face and his hands extended, as he whispered the word, "Lord". She said his last week was his best week ever!

But don't fight God's agenda:

Even a saint needs encouragement

The Psalms are often read for encouragement. Our firefighter was reading from the book of Psalms at the hospital bed of a dear saint from his church who was terminally ill. However, the medication was pulling hard on the man's eyelids. As he slipped off to sleep the patient in the adjoining bed asked our firefighter a question: "David, who wrote the Psalms you read was a Jew, wasn't he?"

"Yes"

"I've always wanted to know where the Jewish nation began."

Our firefighter rattled off the bloodline of Jesus Christ beginning with Adam, then Seth, Enos, Cainen, Mahalal, Jared, Enoch, Methuseluh, Lamech, Noah (the flood), Shem, Arphaxad, Selah, Ebber, Peleg (nations dispersed at the Tower of Babel), Reu, Serug, Nahor, Terah, Abram, Isaac, and Jacob (who was later named Israel). Jacob's twelve sons formed the twelve tribes of Israel.

While he was in the middle of this discourse family members, a nurse, and an attendant were filing into the room and making themselves comfortable when they collectively heard a voice coming from our firefighter's friend, eyes still glued shut, and in a heavy, Italian accent saying "You no fineesha yet!" (You didn't finish yet!)

Our firefighter looked about at everyone in the room who were vigorously nodding. "Well", he said, "From Jacob came Judah and from the tribe of Judah came the Christ child that all Israel was waiting for. He was born in a manger, not only to one day redeem the nation Israel, but also to redeem the world. We call the first event 'Christmas' and the second event 'Easter'. All of us have sinned; therefore all of us need a Savior. All who believe the good news in repentance will find that their sins have been nailed to the cross at Calvary."

There was a smile and a nod of approval coming from the head on the pillow. What the Psalms didn't do, the history lesson accomplished! Jesus is real. He *is* a historical being, and yet He transcends history. That is encouraging.

GRACE TO THE HUMBLE

A Paradigm Regarding Humility

Can you see a pattern emerging? It is truly a humbling process. That's why God opposes the proud, but gives Grace to the humble. (James 4:6, Pro v. 3:34, 1 Peter 5:5)

HOW DOES THIS FIT OUR PARADIGM, "THE LAW OF FAITH?"

THE PROUD PERSON IS...
 SELF- conscious
 SELF- seeking
 SELF- aggrandizing
 SELF- righteous
 SELF- confident
 SELF- reliant
 SELF- focused
 SELF- pleasing
 	
 Summary = SELFISH/ self-centered
 	
 TRUST SELF
 	
 Faith (in self) ....GRACE is blocked
 	
 Work of SELF
 TRUST IN **SELF** GROWS
 	
 PRIDE GROWS
 	
 FALL OF THE PROUD
	THE HUMBLE PERSON IS...
	 GOD- conscious
	    Seeking God
	    Aggrandizing God
	    Righteousness from God
	    Confident in God
	    Reliant on God
	    Focuses on God
	    Wants to please God
	
	 Summary = God-centered
	
	 TRUST GOD
	
	 Faith (in God)...accesses....God's grace
	
	 Work of GOD
	 TRUST IN **GOD** GROWS
	
	 HUMILITY GROWS
	
	 GRACE TO THE HUMBLE

FAITH/GRACE/HUMILITY

Humility = Faith in God

Pride = Faith in self

Proverbs 3:34: "He mocks the proud" (someone with faith in self), "But gives grace to the humble" (someone with faith in God).

James 4:6: "That is why Scripture says: 'God opposes the proud but gives grace to the humble'."

I Peter 5:5: "All of you clothe yourselves with humility toward one another, because 'God opposes the proud but gives grace to the humble'."

Football Illustration

Player A scores and says: "I am the greatest" and spikes the ball.

Player B scores and points his finger on high.

Both accomplish 6 points.

Did they both receive grace?

How does I Peter 5:5 (etc.) apply?

How does faith enter in? (Faith accesses Grace, Romans 5:2)

Player B points up because he **believes** "All good things come from above" (James 1:17); "Who makes you to differ from another" (1 Corinthians 4:7); "I can do all things through Christ who strengthens me" (Philippians 4:13); etc., etc., etc. <u>This faith accesses the grace</u> which is not necessarily the touchdown, but rather the spiritual blessing, i.e. "humility", increased faith, and a testimony for God.

The bigger question is:

WHAT IS PLAYER B *BECOMING*?

and

WHAT IS PLAYER A *BECOMING*?

Player B's faith in God accesses the grace of God in his life, and God does the work of humility, causing more grace and causing more faith, which is causing more humility...on and on.

Player A's faith is placed in himself, leading to pride and resulting in more "self" effort, resulting in a greater reliance on self, fostering a humanistic philosophy, and resulting in a fall regardless of the touchdown. In fact, the touchdown may be adding to the process of the fall.

74

Matthew 18:2-4: "And calling forward a child He set him in the midst of them and said: 'Truly I say to you except you turn and *become* as children by no means may you enter the kingdom of heaven. He who therefore will *HUMBLE* himself as this child this one is the *greater* in the kingdom of heaven."

Mission Impossible

The marble in a peg hole is much more difficult to move than the free-rolling marble. As pride is being stripped off, it becomes easier to be *a tool that is picked up in the Hand of God,* than to be a hand that picks up God's tool (Scripture, etc.). Therefore, when our firefighter was told by the church receptionist, "My uncle is in the hospital and fading quickly. His brother and sister just called me. They are sitting by his bedside now. They are very guarded when Jesus is the subject of conversation. None of them have even attended their own church for years." He took route and was confident but not in his own abilities. Jesus did not walk this earth in silence. He always had something to say to whoever would listen, so our firefighter was sure He had something to say to not only the dying uncle, but also to the brother and sister who sat vigil. And say it, He did! He actually said it to *four* people, because the firefighter felt more like an attentive listener than a purposeful speaker! He was kneeling and stooped at the bedside in order to be at eye level with the patient who could squeeze a hand, once for "yes" and twice for "no".

"Will you pray the Lord's Prayer with me?" One squeeze and an inaudible whisper.

The firefighter recited: "OUR FATHER WHO ART IN HEAVEN... John 1:12 says that you must receive and believe in the name of Jesus to call God your "Father"; do you believe in the name of Jesus to call God your Father? Do you believe Jesus is the Son of God?" One squeeze.

"HOLY IS YOUR NAME... Do you believe that God is perfectly pure without blemish?" One squeeze.

"THY KINGDOM COME... The Bible says that God's Son Jesus will return and set up an eternal kingdom; do you believe and look forward to this?" One squeeze.

"THY WILL BE DONE ON EARTH AS IT IS IN HEAVEN... Are you ready to surrender your will completely to God?" A pause, and then a long squeeze.

"GIVE US THIS DAY OUR DAILY BREAD AND FORGIVE US OUR TRESPASSES AS WE FORGIVE THOSE WHO TRESPASS AGAINST US... Think hard on this because you are asking God to forgive you just as you forgive others. Whoever comes to your mind must be forgiven as you would like your Heavenly Father to forgive you." A longer pause and then a long squeeze.

"AND LEAD US NOT INTO TEMPTATION BUT DELIVER US FROM EVIL... Will you trust God to deliver you from the evil one?" One long squeeze.

"FOR THINE IS THE KINGDOM AND THE POWER AND THE GLORY FOREVER... Do you recognize but one King of Kings, Who is all-powerful and deserves all the glory forever?" One squeeze that would not let go.

Our firefighter asked one final question: "Are you looking forward to meeting your Lord face-to-face?" The strongest squeeze of them all!

It was a twenty-minute ride back to the church. The receptionist was waiting to tell the firefighter that her uncle passed on while he was en route, and the uncle and aunt expressed their gratitude. Only God knows what was going on in the uncle's heart. But only God was in control of the uncle's length of days, hours, and minutes of life. He lived just long enough for the visit!

One thief on the cross next to Jesus chided Him one moment (Matthew 27:44) and believed Him to be Lord the next moment (Luke 23:42). What went on in his heart in this short space of time? This orchestra Leader, God, leaves nothing to chance, and His arrangements are perfect, with each instrument coming in at the precise time He intended! There will be no "oops" in eternity!

Our firefighter reflected on the candle in Mark 4:21. The candle is not light. It does not reflect light, but in the proper environment it will harbor, support, and house light, and the light will illumine all that surrounds. The candle is brought somewhere and is not to be hidden. Our firefighter felt like a candle that was brought somewhere and then was lit. Oh, but what an extraordinary contrast between he and a candle! The longer a candle harbors the flame, the more it wanes. The longer a believer harbors the flame, the more he waxes strong in <u>faith</u>, <u>humility</u>, and therefore, <u>maturity</u>.

The Bushel (Choices)

That candle light annoys us.

That light we now shall tame.

But the more darkness that we produce

The brighter grows that flame.

OR

My light is causing trouble.

I dare not to offend.

There is a way to give them peace;

A way I can amend.

I'LL COVER IT!

Frank L. Sarcone

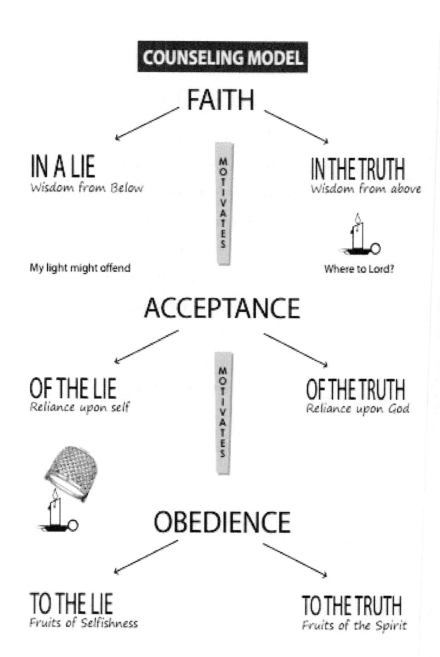

CHAPTER NINE: CANDLES TRUST GOD FOR DIRECTION

In one sense, the "Law of Faith" is a book of application i.e.

FAITH APPLIED PRODUCES:

GOD'S DESIRED WORK

("Which has already been prepared that we should walk in it." Ephesians 2:10)

CHRISTLIKENESS

(**Becoming** like Christ – absolute faith which produces absolute obedience)

With this in mind, consider the following: Romans 10:17 "Faith comes by hearing."

In a study of the Gospel of Matthew you will notice that many petitions were made to Jesus, and He answers an overwhelming amount of times in the affirmative, "Yes". However, when Martha ("Whom He loved") petitioned Him (Luke 10:38-42), He gave her a resounding "NO!" In this setting Martha was a hand that had picked up "tools" (pots, pans, etc.) and was serving the Lord Himself! She petitioned the Lord to convince her sister, Mary, to join her in serving, but Jesus answered, "Martha, Martha, you are worried and troubled about many things. But *one* thing is needed, and Mary has chosen that good part, which will not be taken away from her" (Luke 10:41-42). The Lord, the greatest Servant of all, said there is something more needful than serving! Mary was sitting at the feet of Jesus, sponging up His every word that poured over His lips, and it was not to be taken from her. Those who sit at His feet tend to become like Him. Joyful obedience will come from a loving heart, and a loving heart will come from sitting at His feet.

Consider this poem:

<u>Sponge Up Jesus</u> (Luke 10:33)

A saturated sponge will drip its substance,

When squeezed out it will pour.

Enriching all within its borders,

Then sponging up much more.

The damp one offers little

But tries so hard to please.

So it sets up many helping programs

To put its soul at ease.

Distractions, worries, troubles, complaining –

Prayers of strife...

When "that good part" is abandoned

These are the way of life.

Frank L. Sarcone

MAKING CANDLES

Feed..	My ---	Sheep ---
With what?	I know them by name	They know Me
The Good News!		They know My voice
READ God's word		

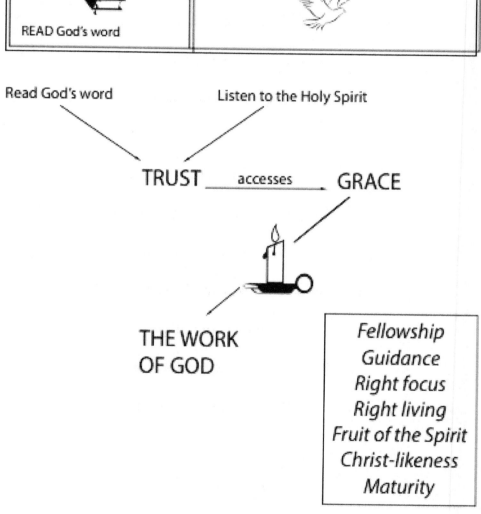

Read God's word   Listen to the Holy Spirit

TRUST ___accesses___ GRACE

THE WORK
OF GOD

Fellowship
Guidance
Right focus
Right living
Fruit of the Spirit
Christ-likeness
Maturity

84

God's Timing God's Way

Does it matter which "candle" God chooses to use? I will let you decide for yourself, but not without a little help.

Our firefighter was now an ordained minister and therefore, he would accompany the prison ministry team on communion Sundays to the local prison where he would deliver a message to commemorate the "Lord's Supper." One member of the team (a senior woman) developed a sincere burden in prayer for a young prisoner. She would encourage him each week, and finally was used by God as the instrument of his salvation. This was a woman who was known to be steadfast in prayer. In fact, she had been praying daily for many years for a little orphaned boy whom she and her husband had hosted for a Christmas many years ago. Once the weekend was over, he returned to the orphanage and they never saw him again. They had bought the little boy a cowboy outfit, complete with chaps, double-holstered six shooters, and a ten-gallon hat. On one of the visits to the prison tears flew from her eyes as quickly as screams of joy from her lungs, when the prisoner produced a photo of that same Christmas visit of yesteryear! That's correct, the little cowboy and the young prisoner were one and the same! She had been praying for his salvation for years, and without realizing it, she herself was the "candle" that God used to bring it about!

Question #2: Who do you think was rejoicing the most? I'm sure it was the Lord!!! How does God orchestrate such things?!

"A QUIP FROM OUR FIREFIGHTER
ONLY GOD CAN USE A TRUE PERFECT TENSE"

← HIND SIGHT   ↑ ↓ NOW SIGHT   → FORESIGHT

God sees all of our YESTERDAYS
God sees all of our TODAYS } ALL OF THE TIME
God sees all of our TOMORROWS

God sees ⟶ 👁

Peter	Peter	Peter	Peter
The fisherman	The apostle	Denying Jesus	Martyred for Jesus

Saul/Paul	Saul/Paul	Saul/Paul	Saul/Paul
A Pharisee of pharisees	A tyrant A terrorist Murderer of saints	A missionary A leader writing Scripture	An honored saint

Man, on the other hand, see through a time.

Line
Sequence
Progression

The tenses we use are only pertinent to those of us on earth, and are not relative except to our planet/ solar system.

BUT TO GOD

No one is <u>pre</u>destined, we are <u>destined</u>.
No one is <u>fore</u>known, we are <u>known</u>.

The Words:
It *DID* happen
It *IS* happening
It *WILL* happen

We open these tenses as we would open compartments. We open them one at a time, and in a definite order. These compartments are always open before God. He can arrange and manage any compartment at any time in order to bring about His desired will.

It sounds like I know what I am talking about doesn't it? Forget about it! This stuff is beyond me. That's why I keep saying, "How did He do that?"

"THE I AM"

There is no "pre" at all with Me,

And "post" does not exist.

There is only "now" and "forever",

So could you please not insist?

You are destined, not "pre" destined.

You are known, and not "fore" known.

My choices are made now and forever,

And the results are set in stone.

Your attributes are limited;

Your reasonings obscure.

Mine are all infallible.

My motives are all pure.

You peer from underneath the sun,

Where time obstructs your view.

I see the whole in one big swoop,

Where nothing is ever new.

Did you choose Me, before I you...

If there is no "fore" and "after"?

Did I choose you, before you Me?

The thought provokes to laughter.

Without the proper faculties

Your thoughts are prone to wander.

My son, as I have said before,

"Some things are too great for you to ponder!"

Give up the ghost!

Frank L. Sarcone

CHAPTER TEN: PONDERING THE TAPESTRY

The brightest "candle" in our firefighter's life was his gal, whom he still called "his bride". She had been praying for her older brother since the wedding that he would not attend in "that church". She had also been spending time with him, more so than ever since he was shut in with a terminal illness. One morning she felt compelled to drop everything and visit her brother. She told the firefighter, "I know I have to talk with him, and I must go alone. Please understand." The firefighter said he would be supporting her in prayer. After about one hour in prayer, the firefighter himself felt burdened to drop everything and join her. He got another one of those "buts" again, i.e. *But, I told her I would wait.* When he was convinced that he should go, he shut the door behind himself just as the phone was ringing. When he considered answering it, thinking it may be his bride, he realized his options were gone. He locked his keys inside their home! Now there was only one direction to go. A surprised, but grateful gal greeted him. Her big brother was so responsive to her, but somewhat hung up on one issue as she explained the gospel (Good News). It just so happens that the issue was the subject matter of this book – The Law of Faith, The Role of Faith. Everyone's eyes welled up as he opened his heart wide to his Lord and Savior, receiving what only grace can offer: forgiveness and eternal life.

The Author = God

The Script Writer = God

The Director = God

The Casting Agent = God

The Producers = God

The Power = God

The cast of characters:

      Candle #1

      Candle #2

      Bronco/Candle #3

      GOD (behind the scene)

      The Voice (was that of God)

PONDER THIS

Matthew 17: 24-27 ... "Throw out your (fishing) line. Take the fish you catch; open its mouth and you will find a four drachma coin. Take it give it to them for My (temple) tax...

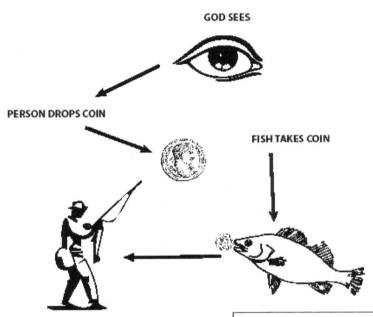

GOD SEES

PERSON DROPS COIN

FISH TAKES COIN

PETER TAKES FISH

John 21:6 "He (Jesus) said, "Throw out your net on the right side of the boat and you will find some fish. When they did they were unable to haul the net in because of the large number of fish."

HOW DOES GOD DO THAT?

Jonah 2:10 "So the Lord spoke to the fish and it vomited Jonah onto dry land."
We cannot see behind the scenes, but that is where the stage of life is set. But what about me? ...Am I aware of His proddings?

Question:

1. Who directed the man that dropped the coin? Why?

2. Who directed the fish?

3. (We know who directed Peter.)

4. How was this staged and timed by God?

5. Why did it happen?

6. Does this apply to my life? How?

"Such Were Some of You": Behind the Scene

A pair of candles (a married couple) were given bonus air miles, when they passed up their scheduled flight for a later flight where they were seated with a terrified bucking bronco. In flight, God lit these candles, and the bronco was illumined enough to seek out their church when he returned. He was directed to our firefighter who had developed and was shepherding a substance abuse group. The bronco said that he was very successful in business. As a public service, he taught seminars regarding the addictive properties of cocaine, a very destructive drug. He firmly believed what he taught, however he saw himself as an exception to the rule. He was highly successful in everything else, surely he could control the use of this substance.

FAITH

In a lie   In the truth (flee temptation)

While listening intently to the bronco's story, our firefighter could imagine the voice of the serpent in the Garden of Eden: *"You can take the fruit, it will make you wise like God."* The same serpent that tempted Jesus in the desert: *"Bow to me and I will give you all of this."* They were wrestling against principalities and powers and so was this bronco, but although he was physically fit to wrestle flesh and blood, he did not even recognize the serpent as an opponent. You see, he was boarding the plane just after a heated conflict with his wife in an otherwise empty room, when he was lifted from his feet and flung against the wall by a force that was not visible to him. Although he was sporting a $300 per day coke habit, he was prepared to listen, and listen he did. Eventually our firefighter was privileged to preside at the ceremony as he and his wife (two new "candles") renewed their marriage vows.

These stories will be much more fascinating when viewed from the perspective of eternity. Will we be given the mental faculties to follow the intricate details involved with directing these elaborate productions? What can we know now?

The Prodding of the Holy Spirit

Things to ponder: The Receiver and the Sender

<u>The Receiver -</u> In submarine movies the sonar operators need to learn to recognize the distractions (whales, other sea life, etc.) and learn to ignore them. They spend many hours fully focused upon the sounds of enemy ships and friendly vessels. The more quality time spent with the *earphones* the more proficient the operator becomes.

<u>The Sender –</u> GOD

God has written sixty-six books for me to know Him well. I inquire and He reminds me of an answer from Scripture. This dialogue makes me familiar with His voice. I ponder His words and that familiarizes me with His voice. My stillness enables me to remove static from the line. The greater the interest shown in a subject, the more heightened the dialogue. Letting God lead in conversation prepares me to follow His initiative. HOW?

You will get the firefighter's perspective on this shortly. Remember what you have been reading is a result of <u>listening</u> in prayer, and <u>remembering</u>. But what about those people who are not tuned in to God, but like pawns are being moved into position? Remember when our firefighter visited his friend in a hospital (Ch. 8)? What drove the friend's sister to the elevator just as the firefighter exited it? What sense of urgency? What was going on in her mind? Certainly, Peter was not focused on

THE LAW OF FAITH AND THE BUCKING BRONCO

Gentiles when he prayed on the rooftop! Or was he (Acts 10:9)? God gave him a dream/vision of things to come. It was not at all pleasant; in fact, it was distasteful! (Pun intended). Peter followed through and then took it to the Jerusalem church, and all realized it was from God! What about the relatives of our firefighter's friend (page 67)? As the firefighter asked God to remove them, they promptly got up and left. Did God work with a feeling? A thought? Did He remind one of them of an important chore that must be done?

Also, how did God coordinate the actions of the firefighter and the man he met on the beach (page 60)? What feelings or thoughts prompted the man to be there at a desired time? Then there were the single young ladies. What went on in the mind of the single young lady and in the mind of her boss (page 54)? What circumstances were manipulated to place them both in position for God's desired will to come to pass? How did God shuffle the mail to make the "Welcome Back" card appear on the wrong (right) desk (page 55)?

We know that the firefighter's wife describes a nagging sense of urgency to visit her brother, and to go it alone (page 91). It was relentless, but could she have shrugged it off? The firefighter agreed to stay home and pray while his gal was speaking with her brother. After about an hour of prayer, he felt an urgency to go to his brother-in-law's home. It was as though he as being pushed out the door. Just how well may we know the ways of God?

ONE MAN'S PATH

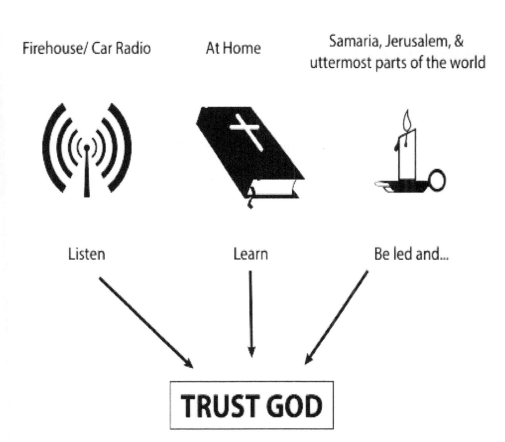

Firehouse/ Car Radio	At Home	Samaria, Jerusalem, & uttermost parts of the world
Listen	Learn	Be led and...

TRUST GOD

THE POWER	THE UNDERSTANDING	EXPERIENCING GOD
Of the Holy Spirit	From the Word of God	Listen and trust and proclaim

Exercising Faith (Refresher)

Just knowing Biblical precepts is not enough! If faith is to have a work, then it stands to reason that faith must be utilized, implemented, made use of, with each decision I make. I prove, show, and demonstrate that I truly believe something when I implement faith in it. Anything else is human logic, wisdom from below, i.e. worldly wisdom.

As often as I exercise faith in God, my mind is being renewed to conform to the mind of Christ, and the <u>love</u> of God grows and shines through as He accomplishes His will through me, to the glory of God.

"They will know we are Christians by our _ _ _ _." (John 13:35)

"Without _ _ _ _ I become as sounding brass." (1Corinthians 13:1)

"But the greatest of these is _ _ _ _." (1Corinthians 13:13)

The first and second commandments sum up all Ten Commandments. "Jesus replied: _ _ _ _ the Lord your God with all your heart, mind and soul. And the second is like it, _ _ _ _ your neighbor as yourself." (Matthew 22:37-39)

"For God so _ _ _ _ed the world that He gave..." (John 3:16)

"For God demonstrates His own _ _ _ _ for us in this, while we were yet sinners, Christ died for us." (Romans 5:8)

"Peter, do you _ _ _ _ Me? Feed/shepherd My sheep." (John 21:17)

"And if anyone gives even a cup of cold water to one of these little ones because he is my disciple, I tell you he will not lose his reward." (Matthew 10:42)

Christ is the picture, the blueprint of what man is meant to be, and one day will be. Without love the blueprint would be remarkably different. A God without love would create a world without love. In the Garden of Eden love of self was prioritized above love of God and love for neighbor (the first and second commandments). Jesus Christ put the train back on track with self–less love. His followers will be known by their L O V E.

CHAPTER ELEVEN: REFLECTIONS

You ***took*** my hand

You ***showed*** me I could trust You with my life and eternal soul.

You ***gave*** me the companionship I could never get anywhere in the world

You ***taught*** me truths not attainable in any classroom or book

You ***made*** life exciting and

You ***made*** death something to look forward to

You ***changed*** my focus, my thirst

People ask – "Why doesn't He do this *for me?*" That's one thing this book seems to be about! There seems to be two prevailing mindsets that hinder this process:

1. THE PUPPET MINDSET – God is the marionette; He pulls all the strings; I am docile.

2. THERE ARE NO STRINGS ON ME – I must do, do, do for God.

Neither of these mindsets requires good communication with God.

Neither fosters companionship with God!

Neither harbors gratitude.

Neither increases love/ joyful obedience.

Neither allows the relationship to grow.

Relationships With God

God sees us and calls us into different relationships with Himself at different times. For Example:

<u>God/Believer as...</u>

*Husband/Wife

Ephesians 5:23, 25.

*Brother/Brother, Sister

Hebrews 2:11.

*Friend/Friend

John 15:15.

*Master/Slave

1 Corinthians 4:1.

Each human relationship requires a level of communication and companionship to be worthwhile. **_Each_** of these is to help us understand our relationship with God, **_not_** **_just one_** *of them!*

Check out the relationship of the apostle John with the Jesus who discipled him while on earth (John 13:23-25),

-vs

The Jesus John met in the book of Revelation (Revelation 1:7).

BOTH ARE TRUE

When asked, "Is there a third mindset?" the firefighter answers, "Perhaps this is one reason for these reflections. If so, I imagine it will take the whole book to begin to describe it. Maybe we will all get closer by its end!"

GOD SEES

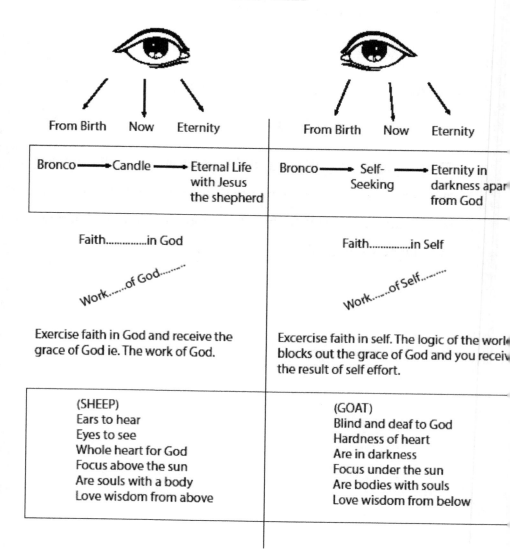

From Birth	Now	Eternity		From Birth	Now	Eternity
Bronco ──→ Candle ──→		Eternal Life with Jesus the shepherd		Bronco ──→ Self-Seeking ──→		Eternity in darkness apart from God

Faith..............in God

Work......of God........

Exercise faith in God and receive the grace of God ie. The work of God.

Faith..............in Self

Work......of Self........

Excercise faith in self. The logic of the world blocks out the grace of God and you receiv the result of self effort.

(SHEEP)	(GOAT)
Ears to hear	Blind and deaf to God
Eyes to see	Hardness of heart
Whole heart for God	Are in darkness
Focus above the sun	Focus under the sun
Are souls with a body	Are bodies with souls
Love wisdom from above	Love wisdom from below

<u>WHAT IS GOD LIKE?</u>

"God Hates Divorce" (Malachi 2:16)

When Truth is re-defined...................Grace is blocked

Work = results in man's work

She was preparing for bed pondering the words of her counselor, "Divorce the bum and get on with your life," and then she saw the face of our firefighter in her mind as her eyes closed. "I wonder", she thought, "If he is still counseling." He was. She went... and within a month's time she and her husband, two love birds, were vibrant in Christ, vital in ministry, and inseparable.

Did she have good reasons for divorce? The world would say a resounding, "YES!" When watching someone suffer, it becomes easy to redefine God's choice. Pastors have to struggle with this. The books they read redefine GRACE. They say, "God is a grace-giving God who certainly would not demand that you suffer like this," rather than knowing a God who would give you GRACE to remain in a bad situation.

Faith is re-defined.............................Grace is blocked

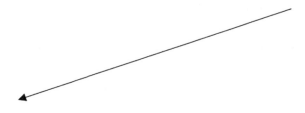

Work = man's work

FOR BETTER OR FOR WORSE

FOR RICHER OR FOR POORER   UNTIL DEATH

IN SICKNESS OR IN HEALTH

Without this in mind they begin to read Scripture seeking loopholes rather than its original intent. They read creatively rather than objectively. They write books and others read them and use them as a basis to write their own books or their own sermons. Creative, subjective matter is accepted as TRUTH and OBJECTIVE FACT, and the procession of caterpillars lengthens its circle and starves to death despite the food that is close within sight. *"There is a way that seems right to a man, but the end of it is death."* (Proverbs 14:12) In this case it could have been death to a marriage!

A Prevailing Mindset

"I married a dreamboat," the young lady said.

A knight in shining armor was he.

His armor had a chink or two, or maybe even three.

But things like that don't really bother me.

In time he'd be what every knight should be.

I hammered on those chinks to find

They just kept getting worse,

Till life was just unbearable to share.

The divorce was even harder, our two kids now dispersed.

Oh, look! Isn't that another knight over there?

I hear he has a chink or two, but that's alright with me.

In time he'll be what every knight should be.

Frank L. Sarcone

"Few And Far Between"

What are we saying?

What is now "few and far in-between" was once commonplace. What was once commonplace is now "few and far in between".

Our firefighter visited a dear saint who was hospitalized. Immediately he sensed the Presence of God in her room. He was not going to give anywhere near the encouragement that he was about to receive, and he knew it! She reminisced from the time she invited her Lord Jesus Christ to be her Lord and Savior. She was married with young children, and her husband and parents strongly protested her "new religion". She was not welcomed any longer into her parent's home, and her husband kept her on a tight leash for fear that she would enter one of those "born-again" churches. The angrier and more hostile they became, the more loving and giving she grew.

In a local church she was called, "the shopping bag lady" because she would time her Wednesday night food shopping to be on time for the pastor's message. There she would sit in the last seat in the last row with bundles of groceries and leave immediately after the final prayer, lest her husband become suspicious. For more than forty years she was an outcast, while she continued "heaping coals" (Proverbs 25:21-22).

Time in that hospital room seemed to stand still as she recounted more than forty years of her life. The firefighter had seen the fruit of her life, and now he had the story of the fruit. Oh how he yearned to see the back-side of the tapestry of those forty years! He was present when her husband (the oldest person ever to be baptized in his church) gave his testimony. Our firefighter was one of the staff of pastors shepherding her children, her children's children, and their children, as the dominos fell one by one. Our firefighter looked into her face from a classroom and a pulpit many times, not realizing the depth of the person behind the kindly smile. Now they switched places and he was blessed more than he could ever have been a blessing to her!

The back-side of a tapestry is a maze of threads seemingly going nowhere in particular. But they all have very definite purpose. When mercy is given to someone who is not exercising Faith in God, is it given because someone else is praying in Faith for him/her? When mercy is given to a "thousand generations" is it a result of the Grace of God through Faith of one of His saints? Do *you* know?

There is a "Law of Faith", but is there a "Law of Mercy"?

It appears that God will give mercy to whomever He wishes (Romans 9:15). When Faith is exercised, Grace is accessed (Romans 5:2). When Faith is not exercised, Mercy may be given, or it may not be given. Obviously, God is not whimsical; therefore it stands to reason that He will apply all of His attributes when making any decision, and He will have good reason for each decision, whether or not I recognize the wisdom or justice that prevails.

BUT: His Word says that Mercy prevails to the bronco in the form of Grace when he exercises Faith in God. Hebrews 4:16 states: "Approach the throne of Grace with *confidence* (i.e. Faith) so that we may receive Mercy and find Grace to help in time of need."

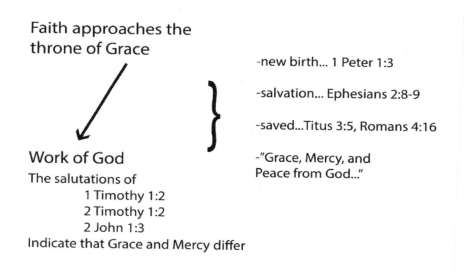

Faith approaches the throne of Grace

-new birth... 1 Peter 1:3

-salvation... Ephesians 2:8-9

-saved...Titus 3:5, Romans 4:16

Work of God
The salutations of
    1 Timothy 1:2
    2 Timothy 1:2
    2 John 1:3
Indicate that Grace and Mercy differ

-"Grace, Mercy, and Peace from God..."

In 1 Timothy 1:3, the apostle Paul says that he was shown Mercy BECAUSE he acted in *ignorance* (believing a lie) and *unbelief* (the absence of Faith). The absence of Faith in God is

Faith in a lie. Therefore, <u>no</u> Faith = <u>no</u> access to Grace apart from Mercy. When Grace is blocked, Mercy may or may not take place (Romans 9:15), but God gives a measure of Faith to everyone. Paul believed a lie which he accepted as truth, and God in His Mercy opened his eyes to the Truth. From that moment on Paul continually exercised Faith in the truth and accessed the Grace of God.

Remember:

Faith in God = Trusting God to do His work/will in the situation.

Grace = God's working out His will through Faith.

(Ephesians 2:8-9   Salvation is by Grace through Faith.)

Sanctification = The just/righteous person shall <u>live</u> by Faith

I repeat, the back-side of a tapestry is a maze of threads seemingly going nowhere in particular, BUT they all have very definite purpose. When Mercy is given to someone who is not exercising Faith in God, is it given because someone else is praying in Faith for him/her? When Mercy is given to "a thousand generations" is it a result of the Grace of God through the Faith of one of His saints? Furthermore, is God inciting that prayer?

<u>Song: Grace Through the Ages</u>

You walked together with Enoch that great man of old

A kindred-spirit was he.

How I yearn to hear the stories that Enoch was told

As he sat right down at Your knee.

Oh the grace displayed to a mere mortal man

Oh the grace that Enoch has known.

Oh the grace displayed to a mere mortal man

The day You walked Enoch home.

Methuselah and Lamech had passed on to glory

Just one kindred spirit was found.

Though the remnant was small as the Lord tells the story

And no record of rain touched the ground,

Father Noah and family were cherished indeed

And saved from the earth's first storm.

How I yearn for the stories that Noah was told

When You kept his whole family from harm.

CHORUS

Five generations from Babel when nations were formed

A kindred spirit was sought.

You formed Your nation from a man named Abram

Whom You nurtured, loved, and taught.

How I yearn for the stories that Abram was told

When You made him the father of Israel.

How I yearn for the stories told that great man of faith,

Those stories I wish You would tell.

CHORUS

Son of Jacob was Joseph, kept from injury and harm

When his family had treated him wrong,

You gave fame and position in a hostile land,

Though to learn he had suffered long.

How I yearn for the stories that Joseph was told

With visions to comfort his soul.

How I yearn for the stories that Joseph was told

As he unraveled mysteries of old.

CHORUS

Then there was Moses, a babe in a basket.

You chose him to lead Israel home.

His face shone with Your glory as You met face-to-face

Although two stints in a desert, he roamed.

How I yearn for the stories that Moses was told

As you carefully planned out his life.

How I long for the stories that Moses was told

To deliver Your people from strife.

CHORUS

Then there is David a great king of the land,

And Daniel and so many more.

The list of great stories is long as you see,

And who knows what God has in store?

But the list will not stop till that glorious day

When all saints are where we belong.

No the list will not stop till that glorious day

The day we will all sing this song!

Oh the grace displayed to a mere mortal man,

Oh the grace Your children have known!

Oh the grace displayed to a mere mortal man,

Praise God, by Your grace, we are home!

Frank L. Sarcone

ENTERING INTO GOD'S REST
HEBREWS 3:4

"For one who enters into God's rest also rests from his works, just as God did from His works"...Heb. 4:10

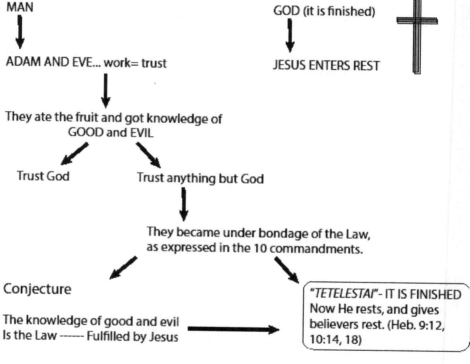

MAN

↓

ADAM AND EVE... work= trust

↓

They ate the fruit and got knowledge of
GOOD and EVIL

Trust God   Trust anything but God

↓

They became under bondage of the Law,
as expressed in the 10 commandments.

Conjecture

The knowledge of good and evil
Is the Law ------ Fulfilled by Jesus

GOD (it is finished)

↓

JESUS ENTERS REST

"*TETELESTAI*"- IT IS FINISHED
Now He rests, and gives
believers rest. (Heb. 9:12,
10:14, 18)

Adam & Eve would have one day entered the rest of God
and eaten of the Tree of Eternal Life IF they continued
their trust of God.

Heb. 3:18 - 19 TRUST AND OBEDIENCE ARE SYNONYMOUS

Heb. 4:16 "Let us then approach the throne of Grace with
Assurance (faith) so that we may receive Mercy and find
Grace to help in time of need."

F...accesses...G

W

<u>Christ-likeness = To Endure (Hebrews 3:14)</u>

Our firefighter had an aunt who enjoyed God's company very much. When she thought she was alone you would hear her talking to her Lord as she would chat to a friend. Her husband was an alcoholic, and abusive in many ways, but not with his hands. You see, the firefighter's dad was a boxer, and made it perfectly clear to her husband that one finger laid on his sister, and he would get his ears boxed but good!

Our firefighter's aunt had never even a twinge of a thought of divorce, and there was never the slightest suggestion of divorce from her family and friends. There was a sincere and sacred honoring of her marriage vows to Almighty God that left no room in her mind or in her heart for such "nonsense". Her door was never locked. She was the source of encouragement to all who needed a lift, and there was plenty of need for encouragement during the Depression years, and later when the men were shuffled off to fight in WWII. Years after she passed on to be with her Lord, the firefighter would hear over and over again how much her presence was missed. She was quite an example of endurance.

<u>Christ-likeness = Seeking His Presence (Hebrews 4:16)</u>

When on a deserted highway late at night it is comforting to see a police car in my rear-view mirror, <u>UNLESS</u> I am exceeding the speed limit, or I am otherwise illegal. In such cases I am avoiding the police, and the presence of a uniform is anything but comforting. The candle that is avoiding God's Presence hides from the illuminating light, and the companionship of his Maker. "Such were some of you." The bronco was becoming a candle that was ever more anxious to be taken to a new lamp stand each day, anticipating the light that illumined him as well as his surroundings. He found himself doing more and more counseling/discipling, as his fellowship with God grew in intimacy. Not many things in God's creation intrigued him more than that which motivates inappropriate responses to circumstances and situations in a person's life.

CHAPTER TWELVE: WHAT MAKES ME TICK?

"I Want That"

Nothing was going to convince the young lad that he wasn't being deprived of something good as he watched the firefighter's dad (the lad's uncle) enjoy each cherry-pepper to the fullest. Those shiny, juicy, bright red peppers looked succulent, and he wanted his share. NOW! The firefighter's dad was not the most patient man around, and eventually the young lad found a red cherry-pepper plunged into his mouth.

It APPEARED to be the perfect solution because the consequences were brief to bear, but lingering in thought.

NOT SO WITH EVE!

NOT SO WITH MANY DECEPTIONS IN LIFE!

But there is more than meets the eye here. To help this boy you might:

1. Deal with "LUST OF THE EYE"

2. Deal with lack of understanding

3. Deal with lack of knowledge

4. Deal with lack of experience

The firefighter's dad probably accomplished this by his affirmative action

5. Deal with rights being denied

BUT

6. Until we deal with the boy's lack of trust in the authority who had more understanding, knowledge, and experience than he, we are not approaching the core of the problem.

AND

7. Unless we can determine <u>why</u> the lack of trust in this authority, we are not <u>at</u> the core of the boy's problem.

The firefighter's dad was a trustworthy man, but the young lad's dad was a very deceptive man. It might chart something like this:

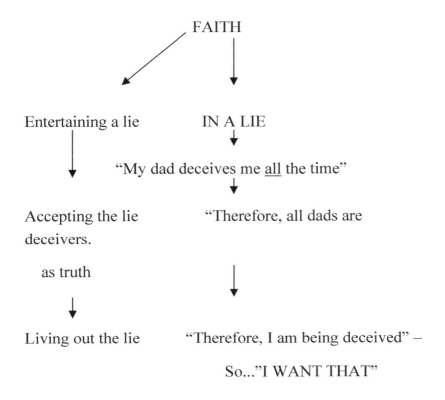

It Can Get Tricky: "Unusual Behavior"

One day the firefighter corrected his son's misbehavior. Ten minutes later he repeated the same misbehavior, and it was again corrected. This was very uncharacteristic of the young boy. Bewildered, the firefighter watched the same misbehavior for the third consecutive time. This time when the boy was taken to his room the firefighter sat him down and said, "Tell me about it, son."

"What, dad?"

"You know son; why are you so different?"

"Well, dad, I was telling my friend that I will be four years old in a couple of weeks, and when you are four you don't need to be corrected so much anymore. My friend said, "Who told you that? When you are four you get more spankings than you ever got in your whole life!"

The firefighter said, "Son, your friend is two years older than you and is very wise, but look at my grey hair. Do you think I may be even wiser than he?"

His son said, "Oh sure dad, you are wiser than he!"

They talked, and the pattern was broken.

The more times the firefighter corrected his son, the more he was reinforcing the friend's wisdom, until the lie was put to rest. Why was this approach so successful? Because the boy <u>trusted</u> his father, and firmly believed he was a truth-teller and that he had the boy's interest at heart!

God uses the Law of Faith to make candles out of bucking broncos. He wants me to be like Him! He is a truth-teller, and He has proven He has my interest at heart. The chart we are using (Page 28) is a great aid toward this end. It helps locate the real problem and to understand its source and solution.

Defining the Problem

A staff of pastors was assembled for lunch and ministry planning. When discussing the direction of the church one pastor (our firefighter) challenged the focus of discipleship. He believed that the church's focus had been to lead new believers, as quickly as possible, to be "Doers" for Christ, and suggested that more time be spent developing "Becomers". Those who *become* more like Christ will do for Him, but those who *do* more for Christ are not necessarily *becoming* more like Him.

No one understood the difference. No one could imagine the process involved. The subject ended as abruptly as it had begun.

WHAT IS THE DIFFERENCE BETWEEN <u>BECOMING</u> AND <u>DOING</u>?

<u>FACTORS</u>

<u>DOING LIKE</u> <u>JESUS</u>		<u>BECOMING</u>
I copy/mimic	OR	I become like
I am a play-actor	OR	I am metamorphosed
I am programmed	OR	I am being made new
I am a look-alike	OR	I am alike
I need a script	OR	Just be the new me

DOING

I am out of my comfort zone

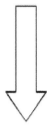

Will this lead me to be like Jesus?

Maybe…or maybe not.

It depends upon other factors.

OR

BECOMING

I am in my new comfort zone

Will this lead me to do what Jesus would do?

ABSOLUTELY

He is Righteous
Holy
Just
Blameless
Etc., etc., etc.
As I become like Him I will see the fruit of these character traits.

Perhaps what we are wrestling with here is the question, "How does God use the Law of Faith to make "bucking broncos" into "candles"?

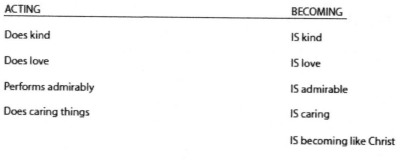

ACTING	BECOMING
Does kind	IS kind
Does love	IS love
Performs admirably	IS admirable
Does caring things	IS caring
	IS becoming like Christ

FAITH
Trust God and...

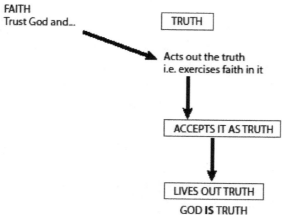

TRUTH

Acts out the truth
i.e. exercises faith in it

ACCEPTS IT AS TRUTH

LIVES OUT TRUTH
GOD **IS** TRUTH

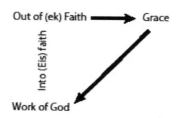

Out of (ek) Faith ➔ Grace

Into (Eis) faith

Work of God

Am I acting like Christ? or... Am I becoming like Jesus?
Acting focuses upon appearance.
Acting may help to develop skills/ performance.
Acting may produce practical helps.

Becoming focuses upon essence...
Develops a similar mindset
Develops character
Develops goals

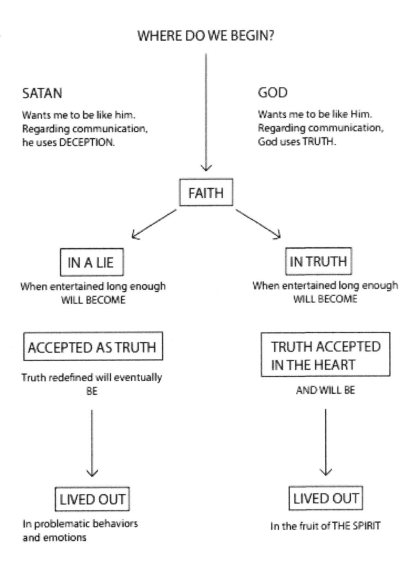

Chart Explained

When truth is revealed it exposes the lie that self has adopted as truth. When truth is exercised enough it is accepted as truth and my behavior changes to conform to that truth, and I have become different. When I truly believe I do not merely act differently; I am different ("Faith without works is dead").

Ponder the chart with me for a moment. The bottom left contains the problematic behaviors and/or emotions that a client would desire to change. The bottom right is what he/she would like in its place.

BUT

The path to change is not a lateral path. It is a path up... and around... and down.

Some marriage seminars are arranged to change behaviors in partners, i.e. they direct couples to travel from bottom left on our chart laterally, to bottom right. In other words the hope is that encouraging behavioral change alone will heal the relationship. My observation is that temporary change takes place immediately, but lasts two to three weeks before they are "doing what comes naturally" again.

Remember, "We wrestle not against flesh and blood, but against principalities and powers", but "The Truth will set us free". Free from what? The lies we have bought into come straight from the pits of hell, straight from the Deceiver himself who works overtime with your "self" to claim you as his own. Cling to Jesus, hang on to His every word; hang out with Him so often that you think like Him, sound like Him, because you are like Him.

Trust And Obey

Let's try another approach to understanding the chart.

At different times in the past our firefighter had two dogs. Ricky was a boxer and Lady was a mixture of collie and shepherd. These were dogs that would go with him when he walked the beach, or the wooded paths, or even take a ride to the store. Ricky liked to run track when they went to the ball field; Lady loved to flush pheasant when they walked the fields. These were dogs that he had perfect control over without a leash. They were the picture of trust and submission. One would find these traits on the right side of our chart.

"I Did It My Way"

BUT Dusty, his present dog, thinks it is his role in life to rid the world of other dogs. The little half pint walks around like a lion. He protects his family when no protection is needed, and the firefighter has as much control over him as he would over a cat. He is loved as much as Ricky and Lady were, but the family feels sorry for him. He misses out on so much. He was bred in Tibet to call alarm when strangers approach, even at a distance. When he is alarmed, he is doing what comes naturally. Knowing Dusty's tendencies made it easier to help him.

He would never be a golden retriever, but he could be a less suspicious and fearful Lhasa Apso.

When "self" does what comes naturally, it dwells on the left side of the chart. To enter the right side, "self" needs to submit to the truth (i.e. exercise faith in the truth) as given by the Holy Spirit and the Word of God.

The man who lives on the right side of the chart

Psalm One

In A Lie ← Faith → In Truth
Vss. 4-6

"The wicked are not so, but they are like chaff that the wind drives away. Therefore the wicked will not stand in the Judgement, nor sinners in the assembly of the righteous. But the way of the wicked will perish."

Psalm 1:1-5 How blessed is the man who does not walk in the counsel of the wicked nor stand in the path of sinners, nor sit in the seat of scoffers! But His delight is in the Law of the Lord, and in His Law he meditates day and night. And he will be like a tree firmly planted by streams of water, which yields its fruit in its season. And its leaf does does not wither; and in whatever he does he prospers.

THE MIND
Delights in the Word
Meditates on it
Ponders truth

THE HEART
Accepts Truth
Its leaf will not wither
Is firmly planted
Is fed
Is watered

THE LIFE
Lives Out Truth
Prospers
Bears fruit
Sows new life
Is blessed
Does not join sinners

CHAPTER THIRTEEN: SOME OBSTACLES DEFINED

Things can get in the way of becoming like Christ. A counselor looks for:

OVER REACTION

UNUSUAL BEHAVIOR

UNUSUAL RESPONSES

John 21:15-19 gives an example: Peter's <u>unusual responses</u> are not evidenced in the English translations of this passage, but when Jesus asks, "Simon, son of John, do you <u>love</u> Me more than these?", He is asking... *"do you <u>sacrificially love Me</u> more than these?"* This uses a form of the Greek word, "agape".

 Peter answers, "Lord you know that I have *<u>brotherly love</u>* for You." Peter uses a form of the Greek word, "phileo".

Jesus does not address the different answer and merely replies, "Feed My lambs." Then Jesus asks the question a second time, "Peter, do you *<u>sacrificially love Me?</u>*"

Peter again replies, "Yes, Lord, you know that I have _brotherly , or friendship love_ for You." Then Jesus answers, "Shepherd My sheep." Jesus questions Peter a third time. This time Jesus changes up and asks, "Simon, son of John, do you have _brotherly , or friendship love_ for Me?"

Peter was saddened when Jesus questioned his friendship and answered, "You know that I do." Then Jesus said, "Feed My sheep."

Would you call Peter's response unusual? A counselor cannot read these passages without wanting more information. Like a detective, he searches for clues. Since he cannot ask Peter more questions, he cannot draw definite conclusions, but there is enough of a context to stimulate conjecture, and to speculate what might have happened behind the scenes.

Let's act like a movie director and get Peter to reminisce back to the events recorded in Luke 22:28-34. The setting is the "Last Supper". In Luke 22:33 Peter tells Jesus, "I am ready to go with You to prison and to death", but Jesus had already said, "Simon, Simon, behold Satan asked ("exegesato"- begged earnestly, made a commanded request, wants you for himself) for you, to sift you as wheat." Apparently, Satan wants the winnowing fan to blow on Peter to reveal (what Satan believes) that he is not "wheat", but "chaff", i.e. "When I show You that he is chaff,

You will know that he belongs to me, not to You...The chaff is mine!"

If we conjecture further, eaves-dropping on Satan's thoughts, it might go something like this: "I have led His own precious people (Israel) against Him. The High Priest is turning Him over to be crucified. I own Judas; he is in my pocket. Jesus is about to be a mockery, as He dies on the cross, a beaten man. His most loyal subjects will be in confusion and doubt while hiding out in seclusion. Peter, himself, is prophesied to deny Him not just once, but three times. Strike the head, and the body will fall. Things have not been this good since the Garden. So much for 'Thy will be done.' It's My will be done on earth, and one day in heaven! It's party time!"

To paraphrase even further, Satan seems to have said to God, "Peter appears to be yours, but he really is mine! You must let me prove it to You!"

The major issue here is the relationship between Peter and God. Remember where we began our study. Jesus was discussing Peter's relationship with Him, "Peter, do you love Me?" Peter is now "not wrestling against flesh and blood, but against principalities and powers." Peter is in one whale of a wrestling match with Satan himself. He has the proverbial angel of God on one shoulder and Satan on the other. How would I have handled the words, "Firefighter, the rooster will not crow today until you have denied three times that you (even) know Me"?

Let's conjecture that Peter's thoughts might be, "My world is crashing in on me. I am recently told that my Master, my Lord, the One I love the most on earth is departing where I cannot follow... He Who I spent twenty-four/sevens with for more than three years. He is the Leader who healed my mother-in-law, who raised Lazarus from the dead, calmed the threatening storm, and fed the masses, the One from whom pearls of wisdom flowed like a river. He is departing, and now I am to believe this about myself? - I will deny that I know Him? NO! It cannot be!"

Soon, Peter had a chance to prove his loyalty when they came to arrest his Lord. He fought for Him, but Jesus healed the wounded enemy, and within hours Peter was hearing the words of denial coming from his own mouth: "I do not know Him", for the third time, and (in a surreal fashion) while the cock was yet crowing, he looked in amazement toward the place they put his Lord, and Jesus peered straight into his eyes. *The memory will have to burn in his heart forever! Then he had to process the cruel punishment of Jesus as He was hung upon a tree to die.*

In three days Peter got reports from reliable sources that Jesus was alive. He could not believe such reports until Jesus Himself stood before him face-to-face, and now we are round-circle as Peter is again looking into the eyes of Jesus who asks, "Peter, do you <u>sacrificially</u> love Me?" Couldn't it be that his heart wanted to cry out, "Yes! Yes! Yes!", but his head (with the help from Satan) reminded him of the rooster crowing when he peered into the face of Jesus with denial still on his lips? And the only words that would come out were, "You know I love You like a brother/friend." Once he expressed a faith that had no work, which is no faith at all. Now, I am sure, he was riddled with doubt about himself. Perhaps if he asked Jesus, "What do you think of me?", the dialogue would have gone like this:

Jesus – "Who told you Satan wants to sift you, Peter?"

Peter – "You did, Lord."

Jesus – "When, Peter?"

Peter – "Immediately after saying the apostles and I would inherit twelve thrones in heaven over the twelve tribes of Israel. So, my future was secure?"

Jesus – "Peter, did I know that you would deny Me?"

Peter – "Yes, Lord, and You said, 'strengthen your brothers when you return to Me'. You knew I would return, didn't You? You said that You prayed that my <u>faith might</u> be strengthened; I remember now. And even now, as I am reminded of the greatest shame in my life, You also remind me that I am still Yours, when You say, 'Feed My sheep'. There is something about the way You speak of my final days that lets me know that I will one day be faithful to You, even unto death."

Can you feel with Peter? Perhaps this poem will help:

Peter

I was certain I would follow Him
Into the pits of hell.
Stick by His side through fiery darts,
But on that day I fell.
He knew I would deny Him thrice
Before the cock would crow.
Yet, He washed my feet with the eleven
And alone He took the blow.
He asked me if I loved Him
In the way that He loved me.
My heart was screaming, "Yes, I do!",
But my mind could clearly see
The day that I abandoned Him
Unto that lonely tree.
How perfect His forgiveness,
How frail humanity.
Condemned by Law to suffer Hell,
But led by the Spirit to be free.
My strength was not sufficient;
A lesson worth the cost!
Left to my own endeavors,
My soul would still be lost.

Frank L. Sarcone

CHARTING PETER
Luke 24:6-23

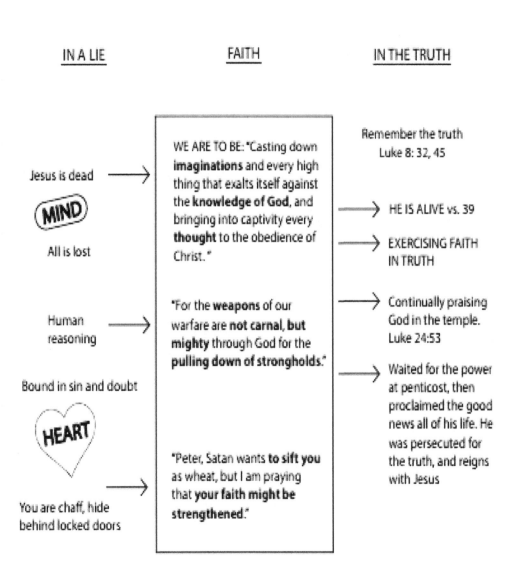

IN A LIE

FAITH

IN THE TRUTH

Jesus is dead

(MIND)

All is lost

WE ARE TO BE: "Casting down **imaginations** and every high thing that exalts itself against the **knowledge of God**, and bringing into captivity every **thought** to the obedience of Christ."

Remember the truth
Luke 8: 32, 45

HE IS ALIVE vs. 39

EXERCISING FAITH
IN TRUTH

Human
reasoning

"For the **weapons** of our warfare are **not carnal, but mighty** through God for the **pulling down of strongholds.**"

Continually praising God in the temple.
Luke 24:53

Bound in sin and doubt

HEART

You are chaff, hide
behind locked doors

"Peter, Satan wants **to sift you** as wheat, but I am praying that **your faith might be strengthened.**"

Waited for the power at penticost, then proclaimed the good news all of his life. He was persecuted for the truth, and reigns with Jesus

GOD'S APPROACH REGARDING THE DISCIPLES

The disciples were dejected and hiding behind locked doors

	FAITH	IN TRUTH
THE WOMEN	Luke 24: 5 "Why do you seek the living among the dead? Remember what Jesus said." Vs. 6-7	Jesus is alive
THE DISCIPLES		He told you this would happen
THE MEN FROM EMMAUS	Luke 24: "Was is not necessary for the Christ to suffer these things and enter into His glory?	Everything is going according to plan as prophesied in the OLD Testament
THE APOSTLES	Luke 24: 38-39, 44 "Why are you troubled?" ... "Why do you doubt?" ...See my wounds; I am resurrected."	I have successfully completed my mission on Earth!
THOMAS	John 20:27 "Put your finger in My hand and put your hand into My side, and BELIEVE."	Whatever it takes to make you believe the TRUTH!
YOU AND I	"BLESSED ARE THEY WHO DID NOT SEE AND YET BELIEVE." John 20:29	

Luke 24: 44-49 It was truth that set them free. Free from what? Free from the wiles of Satan and the doubts of self. But they were free only when the truth was believed and accepted. That is when it began to be lived out!

TRUTH WAS EXPOSED
TRUTH WAS ACCEPTED
LIVES WERE CHANGED This is the counselor's role!

<u>Over Reactions</u>

We have observed that the absence of truth (i.e. more specifically, absence of accepted truth) shows up in "unusual behaviors" (Page 123), as well as "unusual responses" (Page 134). Now let's try to demonstrate how believing a lie shows up in "over reaction."

Her husband insisted it was time his wife sought help for her problem. For years she was having bouts of depression that only lasted for a few days, or at most one week. Through a series of questions our firefighter brought her back to those events and the context of each. It was determined that each depression began with feelings of guilt associated with some minor infraction at her office or in her social setting. However, her response in each matter was text-book. She confessed when appropriate, made restitution, etc., yet her heart was heavy-laden and she became depressed. She over-reacted to each problem. When she should have felt this much guilt (), she was feeling this much guilt (   ). Each incident was merely a catalyst that drew a pipeline to a much larger well of guilt inside of her. Further questions brought out the source of guilt that needed to be dealt with. In this case, when a young child, she had taken on a responsibility that God had never given her, and she could never have handled. Her guilt was irrational. Now that the <u>lie</u>

from hell was exposed, she could deal with the real problem instead of the catalyst.

Whenever she began to feel guilty she could put it all in perspective, <u>remember the truth,</u> and cut off the pipeline to a phantom well of guilt, and deal with the minor infraction.

<u>Gunnysacks</u>

Over-reactions also stem from "gunnysacks" which are often the cause of major conflicts and arguments in relationships. So, what is a "gunnysack"? It is a term once used to describe the luggage that a soldier was issued. It is a cylindrical canvas bag, and when filled is large enough to fit into it a soldier's every belonging. But obviously, our firefighter uses the term differently, i.e. a "gunnysack" is the place we put our every unresolved conflict.

Perhaps a short story will be our best definition –

With her new central vacuum system she was vacuuming their bedroom floor when from under his side of the bed a large black sock raced up the nozzle and was barely snatched by her free hand in time. "He is always leaving things where they don't belong! One day that sock will be stuck in the wall", but then, good Christian woman that she is, she said: "What's the matter with me? He is such a good man, and I am going to forgive and forget."

She went on to iron his shirt, but as she grabbed the ironing board, a wrench that he left on it, fell on her slippered foot. "He is going to kill me one day, I don't believe that guy." But true to form, good Christian woman that she is, she said, "There I go again. Lord, I forgive him and I will forget the matter." After breakfast she pulled the toaster plug from the wall, but the bare wire sparked and blew the circuit breaker. "He was supposed to fix that last week; is he trying to electrocute me? Woo, hold on girl, you have a good man there; you need to show some appreciation for him... forgive and forget! I know what I'll do... I will make him his favorite meal to show him how much I love him."

The stove timer went off at 5:55 P.M. He always gets home at 6:00 P.M. The timing is perfect. BUT, the door does not open at 6:00 P.M. The door does not open at 6:30 P.M. The door does not open until the meal is flat and cold, and when he does come in the door, he is greeted by an irate wife who wants to smack him across the face with supper!

Well, what does *he* see? It is the first time he was late in eight months. He stopped to help an elderly lady with a flat tire, in the rain. He could not call home; cell phones were not yet invented! He sees a huge over-reaction to the situation.

What neither of them sees is her gunnysack. She looks like a crazy lady. The ruined dinner, because of his lateness, was merely the catalyst of her reaction. The gunnysack caused the real reaction. But she forgave and forgot! Did she? Some things require reconciliation, or they pile up in your gunnysack and lie in wait for a catalyst to spill out all over the place.

These were two very nice people who developed large gunnysacks that began to block out conflict resolution, and make compatibility seem impossible. If and when they did communicate, they did not communicate toward resolution. At this point they may seek counseling, and the counselor may hear something like this:

Wife – "Your tools... do you have to leave your tools all over the house?"

Husband – "No, if your lazy son would help me finish renovating the bathroom we would have been done already; besides, when we carry them into the basement we will probably trip over your vacuum cleaner that you always leave at the top of the stairs."

THE LAW OF FAITH AND THE BUCKING BRONCO

Wife – "Well, it would be in a closet if you weren't too lazy to make me one."

Husband – "Make you a closet?? I sweat in ninety-five degree weather to make you a closet! It took me an entire weekend, and there is nothing in it but dust! You don't even use it!"

Wife – "Well, any idiot that would build a closet above the cellar steps, where it would take an ox to lug a vacuum cleaner there, deserves to have sweated for a weekend!" It went on like this for a solid ten minutes. At this point, the firefighter asked, "Remind me, what is the conflict you are addressing?" Neither of them remembered. Get the point? They were more interested in airing their gunnysacks, and proving guilt/blame, than resolving the conflict. They sounded like prosecutors in a courtroom before a judge, not lovers in an office before a counselor. They were having a tug-of-war. The trick was to get them both on the same side of the rope, pulling in the same direction.

When this was done, they had the particular issue resolved within ten minutes, but there was still a bulge in each sack that needed reconciling. How does such a bulge take form?

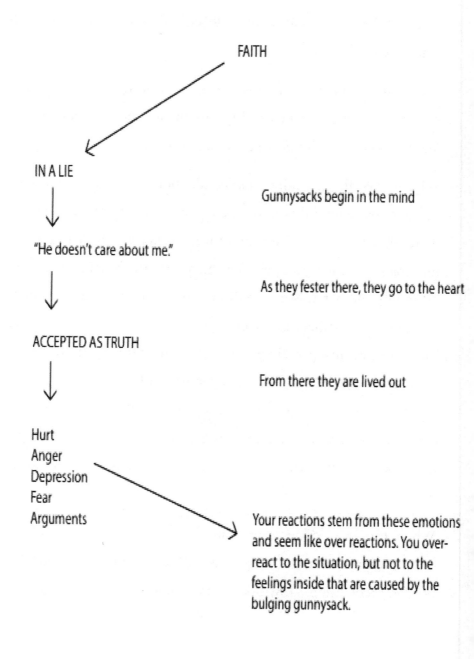

Remember, we wrestle not against flesh and blood, but against principalities and powers. **_Our_** strength does not measure up to every occasion.

Jesus said, "It is not what goes into a man that defiles the body, BUT what comes out of a man." The book of James explains this, using the tongue as an example.

James 3:2-18

Satan/Deceiver   Self-Effort

3:6 - "The tongue is set on fire by hell."
3:14 - The tongue *lies* against the *truth*.
3:8 - No man can tame the tongue.
3:2 - Without exception, if you bridal the tongue the
whole body will also be bridled."

BUT, only Jesus did this. He left us with the solution:

With each decision
Only 2 choices:

TRUST

The Problem   **The Solution**
Wisdom from below: *Wisdom from Above:*

3:14 - lies against the Truth   3:17 - is pure, peaceable, gentle,
                                                                      reasonable, without hypocrisy

3:15 - is earthly, natural, demonic

3:16 - is jealous, selfish, causes disorder   3:18 - sows righteousness and peace

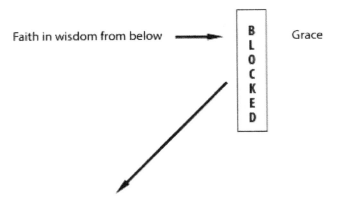

Faith in wisdom from below ➡️ **BLOCKED** Grace

Work= tongue and body out of control

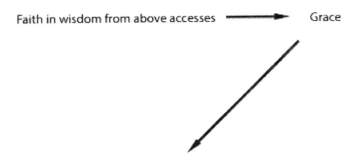

Faith in wisdom from above accesses ➡️ Grace

Work of God. God tames the tongue and is able to tame the whole body.

God tames the tongue and is able to tame the whole body.
BUT

Wisdom from above becomes more difficult to recognize when:
<u>Truths</u> are being <u>redefined</u>:

By – Society

By – The Government

By - The Media

By – Counselors

By – The Churches

<u>Values</u> were being <u>lost:</u>

First-time visitors who had heard that there were helpful people
at "that church", sounded something like this: "I was married to
John, and we had two children, Louis and Jane. We separated
and I began living with Tony who had two children of his own
until we, together, had Michael.

We eventually split up. I divorced John and married Peter. Peter
had two children, but only one was living with him, and Louis

and Jane came to live with us. What do you think would be the *"godly"* thing to do with the child I had from Tony?"

Our firefighter needed a pencil and paper to chart the complicated problems presented. People were not seeking to be like Jesus. They were comparing themselves to one another, and as the morals of society degenerated, they followed the gradient... where surgery was required, band aids became the protocol, even by loving pastors. "RE-DEFINING" fills pews, and pew-filling was being presented as the measure of a "great church".

These people were reading "How to" books that were filling the Christian book stores, and hearing "How to" psychologists who were given prime spots in pulpits and handsomely paid to teach "How to" things at seminars.

Self-reliance began to dominate the churches:

When I exercise **Faith** in God (in truth), I access the **Grace** of God, and God does the **Work**. It is a work of faith, produced by God, and God gets the glory. But when I set out to accomplish a task in my own strength, my faith is in self, and I get the result of self-effort. Self-effort today, has produced a runaway divorce rate, a diminishing of family identity and family values, an overflowing substance-abuse problem, a stream of abortions, and abandonment of children; in short, a tearing of the moral fabric, not only in a once Judeo-Christian country, but in the local churches throughout our world.

Just as water will flow in the path of least resistance, fallen man has followed the path of Adam. But, there is another path! It is a narrow path, and the only path that leads HOME... a path where bucking broncos become candles, and eventually see their Maker face-to-face for an eternity!

Salvation = by **Grace** through **Faith**

Sanctification = the righteous shall live by **Faith**.

Is this YOUR focus?

****

EPILOGUE: THE AUTHOR'S REFLECTIONS

The Bucking Bronco has now been sent to green pastures, where he chews the cud, and observes life through a post and rail fence. His legs do not carry him in the manner they once did, but his ponderings soar!

He observes a fearful church. Some are reluctant to recognize and use the power given at Pentecost. Others are reluctant to exert the energy of faith provided by it, and both are much too tolerant of worldly views. He calls these ponderings:

NEGLECTED GRACE.

Perhaps you will agree!

Today's church tends to focus upon "GRACE", available as pardon for sin, while it neglects to address GRACE that may be accessed for power, direction, and service. In other words, "I sin, and God forgives. That's GRACE". Instead of, "I exercise faith in God, thereby accomplishing the work and will of God" (Romans 5:2).

The focus is on the forgiveness of sin while neglecting the power to overcome and refrain from sin. Even more so, we tend to neglect the ability to hear and to be led by God, as candles being placed upon a lampstand.

The apostle Paul asks, "Should I sin all the more that GRACE should abound?" The reply should be, "God forbid!" (Romans 6:1-2).

Has the believer become so self-centered that he sees only the gift given to him, and not the great cost of the gift to his Savior? If I were to contemplate sinning, shouldn't I also be contemplating the punishment I have added to the Lord when I trample the blood of Jesus, as stated in Hebrews 10:29? Such remorse should lead to conviction, repentance, and a contrite heart that bears true repentance for the blood that I caused to be shed. Do I really appreciate the great cost of the GRACE given to me, or do I feel free to sin against my God, welcoming the GRACE that He paid so dearly for?

When exercised, faith the size of a mustard seed can move a mountain,

BUT

unless exercised, faith the size of a mountain cannot move a mustard seed!

James understood this when he wrote, "But whoever gazes into the perfect Law of Liberty and continues in it, who is not a forgetful listener, but an ACTIVE WORKER, that person will be blessed in his work." (James 1:25)

"So should I sin all the more that GRACE should abound? GOD FORBID!" (Romans 6:1, 2)

BUT

Should I trust more that GRACE should abound?

GOD BE GLORIFIED! Let GRACE abound!!!

Faith is to be exercised so that sin does not abound! (James 2:14-17) So, do I have bragging rights?

"For if Abraham was justified on account of works, then he has something to brag about. But not before God; what does the Scripture say? 'Abraham BELIEVED GOD and it was accounted to him for righteousness.' " (Romans 4:2,3)

God accepts as righteous him that has faith in Jesus, where then does boasting come in? It is ruled out, through what sort of law? Of works? No indeed, but through the Law of Faith; for we come to the conclusion that a man is justified by faith without the works of the Law." (Romans 3:26-28)

Bragging rights belong to Jesus!

Boasting is ruled out through the Law of Faith which accesses the GRACE of God, not only toward pardon for sin, but also for the GRACE that empowers me to overcome and refrain from sin, and to be led by the Holy Spirit whenever and however He chooses.

Legalism *is:* When I trust myself to perfectly keep the Law of God, thereby gaining or earning my salvation, and accomplishing my sanctification.

Legalism is *not:* When I trust Jesus to have perfectly kept the Law for those who exercise enduring faith toward salvation and sanctification. (Romans 3:26-29)

"Righteousness is attributed to those who walk in the footsteps of the faith of Abraham." (Romans 4:12)

Faith is demonstrated by *acts* of faith, and the lack of faith is demonstrated by the lack of the same. Adam and Eve demonstrated a lack of faith in God when they took the forbidden fruit. Cain demonstrated a lack of faith in God when he refused to sacrifice from his flock. Abel demonstrated his faith in God when he heeded God's Word and sacrificed from his flock. Hebrews Chapter Eleven is full of man's demonstration of faith in God. THIS IS NOT LEGALISM!!!

I repeat, WHEN EXERCISED, faith the size of a grain of a mustard seed can move a mountain. UNLESS EXERCISED, faith the size of a mountain cannot move a mustard seed!

Hear His voice and trust His Word. He is worthy!

So... what is this book?

This book is not:	BUT	This book is:
Not about God answering prayer		Is about God's leading in prayer
Not about my will being accomplished by faith		Is about God's will accomplished by the faith He gives me to exercise,
Not about a firefighter or bronco		Is about God, who makes broncos into candles.
Not a "HOW TO BOOK" demonstrated through the events in a firefighter's life		Is a "HOW DOES HE DO THAT?" book

WHY THIS BOOK

This book is a gathering of memories that display the faithfulness of God in the life of a very grateful servant. It serves as a thank you card to his Creator and Lord, "Lest the rocks cry out!"

Psalm 26:7: "That I may publish with the voice of thanksgiving, and tell of all thy wondrous works." Bon appetite!

Made in the USA
Middletown, DE
27 June 2020